Cherries & Lemons

THE USED CAR BUYER'S HANDBOOK

Cherries & Lemons

THE USED CAR BUYER'S HANDBOOK

Joe Troise

South Bend, Indiana

Cherries and Lemons —The Used Car Buyers Handbook
Copyright © 1979 by Joe Troise & and books

All rights reserved. No part of this book may be reproduced or transmitted in any form or by any means, electronic or mechanical, including photocopying, recording or by any information storage and retrieval system, without permission in writing from the Publisher.

and books
702 South Michigan, South Bend, IN 46618

Library of Congress Catalog Number
79-51004

International Standard Book Number
ISBN 0-89708-005-X

First Printing 1979

Printed in the United States of America

Additional copies available:

        and books/the distributors
        702 South Michigan
        South Bend, IN 46618

Don't be fooled by the seemingly insignificant proportions of this book. CHERRIES & LEMONS is, ounce for ounce, more fully packed with valuable information than books weighing up to ten pounds!

When mixed with water, this book will swell to over seven times its normal size. The cover is manufactured of the finest of cardboard stock know to the industry and should withstand a direct hit of a 155 mm artillery shell. Less the front or rear covers, table of contents and page numbers, this book has been officially clocked at over 90 miles per hour,

Please observe all federal and state reader's safety regulations before proceeding to the next pages.

Thank you,

The Author

To Candi,
Fast Eddie Jamal
and
Ol' 55

Contents

	Introduction: In The Defense Of Used Cars	xi
	A Warning From The Author	xix
1	Is There a Lemon in Your Life?	1
2	The Case of the Ravishing Renault	9
3	The Best and The Worst	19
4	Your Finances	55
5	The Search	63
6	Checking It Out	81
7	The Actual Purchase	99
8	Care and Feeding	111
9	Saving Money On Parts and Repairs	123
10	The Automotive Industry and You	141
	Appendix:	
	Questions People Always Ask Me	150
	Autobiographies	155

INTRODUCTION

In The Defense Of Used Cars

Since the publication of an early version of this book in 1977, I have received many comments; almost all expressed the difficulty in deciding whether to buy a new or "used" car. I am convinced, in case you couldn't guess, that, in most situations, buying a used car *is the best way to go,* and here, I present a few details about how and why I've reached this conclusion.

One of the basic, and most convincing arguments against buying any new car these days can be found in the daily newspapers. Have you recently read the automobile advertising that describes how you can buy a new car for *only* "$99 down and $99 per month"? In many cases you may have also noticed that just below the picture of the wonderful new car, there is some very fine print that appears like just a smudge on the paper. With a magnifying glass and eagle-vision, you will learn that those $99 per month payments will continue for 60 long months! In other words, five solid years.

Not only is this longer than most jail sentences, but it's also long enough for many "new" cars of today to become completely worn out. Could you even *imagine* making payments on a car that has to struggle to go around the block, or barely down the road a piece? Yet, this is what you will probably face when you buy a new automobile for $5,400, of which over $1,500 goes to interest payments! Does this sound sensible?

Well, ok, let's assume that you have the *cash* for a new car. In this case you may contend that you're off the credit-treadmill, and buying a new car will avoid all the hassles and repairs that go along with used automobiles. After all, a "used" car is just a headache that someone else got rid of, right? From a mechanic's point of view, I'm not so sure that you are right about that.

Let's take a case in point. Say that in 1971 you bought a brand new Ford Mustang. Your neighbor, the cheapskate that he or she is, bought a used 1965 Mustang at the same time. You paid about $4,000, while your neighbor shelled out maybe $1,200 for the used '65, a pretty clean used car at the time. Now today, as you are reading this book, *both your car and your neighbor's would be worth about the same.* And even if your neighbor spent over $2,000 in repairs through the years, the actual *cost-per-miles-driven would still be in your neighbor's favor!*

Of course, there are still people who won't accept the arguments for buying a used car, and will insist on buying a shiny new one on the grounds that: (1) *new cars are more economical,* and (2) *new cars are less prone to pollute the air that we all breath.* These are both very well-founded points, since new cars are, in fact, generally more economical and cleaner running; so how can I favor buying a used car? Simple.

Introduction XIII

Are New Cars Really More Economical?

Today's car buyers are becoming so thoroughly obsessed with the idea of "good gas mileage" that they are blinded to many other, equally important considerations. For instance, have you ever *actually* calculated, in dollars and cents, the true cost of operating a certain kind of used car as compared to a certain kind of new automobile? For example, let's say that you now own a 1971 Volkswagen bug which delivers about 22 miles per gallon in the city, and perhaps a healthy 28 miles per gallon on the open highway. This little car of yours is getting old and will probably require some major repairs in the near future, so you figure that it's about the right time to buy another small and economical car to replace it.

After carefully scoping out the new automobile market and after some consideration, you choose a Honda Civic. Among other reasons, it is advertised with an EPA (Environmental Protection Agency) gas mileage estimate of *approximately* 40 miles per gallon on the highway. Hey! That's nearly *twice as much* as your old VW was getting, and the car appears quite impressive. That gas mileage almost sounds too good to be true! Well folks, it isn't *exactly* true. In fact, your expectations regarding the savings you will soon be pocketing are going to be far less valid than the ad-hype promises and here's why:

When you start driving that cute little puppy from Japan, although it is indeed a fine car, it won't be too long that you discover that your *actual* gas mileage in city/country driving will be closer to the 30 miles per gallon mark! So then, what happened to the EPA estimate and all that good stuff about saving bucks in gasoline consumption? Can't we trust anyone any longer?

The culprit in this misunderstanding is easily found and is typical of most advertising hype, as well as media distortions in general. If you fail to read the fine print, the fine print will one day return to haunt you, much larger than you ever imagined. That Honda advertisement claims the car's gas mileage as an "EPA Estimate", and if there is *one thing* that the government is never very accurate about, it is in making estimates. Besides, it also is clearly stated there in the ad, something like: "you're actual gas mileage may vary, depending upon individual driving habits and conditions...." Just because the EPA tests cars on a computerized machine, located in a nice warm building, and then, *you* fail to drive according to estimates, does little to change these statistics. The estimates are accurate, it is *you*, the driver, that is messing up. So, perhaps you should spend some time learning how to drive more economically. Or, try getting your new Civic tuned-up to them EPA specs.

Well, you say, trying to console yourself, 30 miles per gallon isn't that bad! So after a period of rationalization, you may conclude that those miles will add up, and *some* savings are better than none. How right you are! After one year, or some 10,000 miles of driving, (at a price of 95 cents per gallon) you will have actually save approximately $80 with your new Honda.

Now, if we compare the new Honda to a 1971 Dodge Dart Six, getting only 17 miles per gallon, you will have saved a whopping $175. Compared to the gas guzzling 1971 Chrysler New Yorker, the new Honda Civic will yield you an annual fuel saving of about $350.

Introduction XV

Even the most basic arithmetic will demonstrate that the money you save on gasoline by owning a thrifty new car cannot justify the initial cost of that little auto. Even in the most extreme case imaginable, let's say a VW Rabbit getting nearly 40 miles per gallon, when compared to the biggest, most obscene, gas-wasting Buick-Oldsmobile-Cadillac Coupe DeVille V-10 Battlecruiser, your annual fuel savings would not be much more than $700 for the 10,000 miles driven. That $700 is just about the amount of depreciation that you will have to endure the *first minute* that you drive your new VW Rabbit out of the dealer's showroom. So, you won't even begin to have a financial advantage over the Cadillac owner for a full year, at which time your new car warranty expires and you will be running the same risk of repairs as any other used car owner.

I could continue on and on about the myth of new cars being fantastic in fuel economy, but I will end here by urging you to realistically examine and calculate the money you will save in gasoline over the average mpg of a good used car (20 mpg). It is likewise important to remember that new cars are far more expensive to insure than used ones and, in most cases, also more expensive to repair. With these thoughts, I hope that the point is made: buying a new, sub-compact car may make sense in terms of scaling down your needs and perhaps improving your good taste, but *it does not "save" you anything.* Only an advertising agency could have the audacity to insist that the *real way to save money is to spend lots more of it*, and the way to solve a problem is to buy something else to cure it!

Do New Cars Improve The Air We Breathe?

Now for the tricky second part of this argument, namely, to dispel the claims about the apparent benefits derived by society if everyone were to trade-in their old cars for newer ones and thus create a better environment (since new cars have more efficient anti air-pollution systtems). On the face of it, no rational dispute seems possible because there is plenty of good hard evidence to *prove* that new cars have significantly cleaner-running engines than do even cars of five or ten years ago. But let's proceed with a statistical approach on this point a little further.

If it is undeniably true that cars are getting cleaner, then it is likewise true that they are getting more and more numerous. Automobile registrations are growing rapidly in the United States, even though we already have enough cars on the road *to carry the entire population of our country twice over!* (the Ultimate Rush Hour). So, what are we accomplishing in buying new cars that pollute the air less? Especially if in doing so, we double the number of automobiles on the road in the next ten years? Where is the great improvement if we replace one old VW with two new ones? And what will "improved gas mileage" mean when most cars will spend a large portion of their time in massive traffic jams? Wouldn't it make just as much sense for many of us to rebuild or better maintain our present cars and perhaps drive them a bit less. Alternatively, we could also encourage the giant automobile industry to research and manufacture more efficient anti-pollution devices for already existing older automobiles.

Introduction XVII

I think that it's really about time for our post WWII consumer-madness to end. It is absolutely crazy to drift along with the manipulations being foisted upon us by the automotive industry and oil companies and their respective advertising media (I say "their" media since it is not a great problem to figure out who really owns much of our vast communications network). In order to sell us more products, auto and oil manufacturers have recently begun sounding like Mahatma Ghandi, explaining how very much they care for our natural environment and how carefully and wisely they have created *exactly what we need* to save us from the perils of pollution and the machinations of the Arab world. Listening to these good corporate vibes, one can almost forget that if it were not for the pioneering efforts of the State of California, Ralph Nader, and, only much later, the reluctant giant we affectionately know as our Federal Government, these very same automobile and oil companies would have been quite content to see us burn all the energy in the solar system and choke ourselves to an inevitable death in the process.

If it is not our feelings of guilt or patriotism that get exploited by car manufacturers, then it is our sense of fear. Already, I am reading ominous warnings from the gasoline producers that before the 1980's gasoline prices will increase to over $1.00 per gallon. The scary tale continues: that in order to *best prepare* for the high fuel cost, I am *well advised* to buy a new car. I *must have* a sparkling new $6,000 mini-car to "survive the realities" of the near future! Alternative choices are few, but fear not, the car industry has a clever suggestion. One may purchase an *even more expensive* diesel-powered car which will surely allow us to "beat the high cost of gasoline". True enough, but beware, it will not do much to beat the high cost of diesel fuel once the price is raised to meet the balance of "supply and demand" — nor will it help to avoid the astronomic costs of repairing a diesel engine.

Often it is what you *don't hear* from the advertising media that can give you an accurate picture of the near future. Oh, certainly, gasoline prices will increase, even beyond the dreaded one dollar level, I guess. But before you lean out of the window of your 1980's gas-saving auto to snicker at your neighbor's gas-guzzler, keep in mind that in recent government tests, brand new cars, driven at a speed of only 5 miles per hour (the speed of a child on a tricycle), sustained as much as $400 damage when run into a test barrier. And also keep in mind that your new car will surely require unleaded gas as do most cars built since 1975. This feature on new cars adds 4 to 10 cents more in cost for every gallon of gas, compared to the regular gasoline burned in older cars.

As for me, I'm not going to play the game any longer! I prefer a different game; one in which I'll simply save $6,000 and pay *myself* the $99 down and $99 per month for only 60 months. In this way I can afford to buy a good, small used car, make it as safe, reliable and clean-running as I can (I'll tell you how to do that later), and still have lots of money left over for perhaps a motor-cycle, bus fare (occasionally), or to join a car pool. Of have my thumb enlarged for hitch-hiking purposes. Of course, I realize that many people do not enjoy the same choices I have, and perhaps even *you* still believe that a new car is the best approach. Certainly, you might be correct, but you should at least think about the famous words of Dealin' Bob Dilman, a used car salesman with the fastest pen east of the Rockies:

"Don't forget folks — every car on the road is a used car!"

A Warning From The Author

Now that I have effectively won you over to buying a used car, I'd like to suggest that the two of us come to a certain understanding. Let's face it, the opinions that I offer in this book are going to be strongly biased in keeping to what I believe to be the right way, the right car, and the right whatever, but it is *your* money that's being spent. So you should have the privilege of knowing how I think, that is, what assumptions I'm making before proceeding with the rest of the material.

First of all, when I claim to know what a *good car* is, I don't mean good handling, good styling, or even good assembly methods of its construction. What I simply mean is a *reliable automobile*, and that, in a nutshell, is all that a *good car* is to me! One that doesn't break down often, is reasonably safe, and gets the job done. The cars that I recommend may not be the most exciting or beautiful automobiles, but so what if your car does not impress anyone, or lacks a spiffy 150 mile-per-hour speedometer? How long are you going to wait to put your toys away anyhow? Being in love with a car is *sick!* (although I must admit being friends with one seems harmless enough).

According to my definition then, are Citroens, Jaguars, Lamborghinis, or Ferrarris *good cars?* Of course not! Beautiful? Yes. Fun to drive? You betcha! Assembled with the greatest care by little old craftsmen in leather aprons? But of course. Marvels of the petro-mechanical technology? Absolutely. But not a one of them would serve you as faithfully as a Chevy taxicab.

Now that's not to say that the only cars I'm going to mention are dull workhorse automobiles. You *can* have your cake and eat it too, provided that you are careful and willing to look at things just a bit differently. But more of that later.

My second opinion in locating a good used car is that *the most reliable cars ever produced in the United States (as well as in foreign countries) come from the era of 1955 to 1975.* So if you're one of those antique car buffs, sorry, you're in the wrong book.

Another basic assumption is that *a car is only worth what it does.* No more, no less! Re-read this because it is a very important point! A used car's value is not always determined by somebody's "blue book." For instance, some used cars are so damn good that they are nearly worth their weight in gold if you could get your hands on one, because they will give you many more years of reliable and safe service.

Finally, in a complete absence of modesty and all humility, I claim that *Cherries and Lemons* is the first and only Used Car Guide that will *not* bore you to tears. It contains valuable information about used car buying, which you will probably not find anywhere else, and, as an investment, should pay for itself many times over.

Cherries & Lemons

ONE

IS THERE A LEMON IN YOUR LIFE?

> Society is divided into two classes: the shearer and the the shorn; we should always be with the former against the latter.
> —Chas. de Talleyrand

Whenever I meet someone with a long sad story to tell about the "lemon" of a used car they got stuck with, I can usually trace the primary cause of the whole sordid mess back to one thing: *they were in too much of a hurry to buy it.*

The act of rushing, of haste, has sort of a passionate, romantic quality to it, but passion and used cars go together about as well as prime rib and jelly beans (I know, kids enjoy things like that, but they don't drive). At least, when you play "true-life romance", once in a while you gamble, but you *can* actually win! However, if you approach a used car emotionally, you are tailgating on the Highway of Destiny and will inevitably face the consequences of your foolish recklessness. You cannot choose a used car as you might a mate or a lover. Rather, choose one as you would a dentist; you know, rationally! In fact,

I once knew someone who chose a dentist passionately, but that is really subject matter for another kind of book.

Ah, you find such advice a bit too cautious? Well, think about it. Why are the most wretched, miserable, rotten, merciless used cars often the same ones you liked best when you first bought them? While we're on the subject of feeling miserable about owning rotten cars, what exactly is a "lemon" anyway? Are they built that way? Do owners create them? Or, is it just a matter of bad luck now and then? Actually, different people have different answers to these questions.

If you listen to various spokespeople for the major automobile manufacturers the world over, you will probably hear that there is no such thing as a *real* "lemon". To them, a lemon is merely a fictitious creation of consumers who know very little about cars, and try to blame whomever they can for what amounts to their own neglect, stupidity, and poor judgment.

To the average car owner, the lemon is a car that constantly breaks down, drains the old pocketbook, and makes driving, a tedious chore at best . . . if not a nightmare. It is a car that is cursed, jinxed, and in possession of a certain dull, yet evil intelligence which seems to permeate the car and resembles something between that of a rock and a snake. A lemon is a car that, although not quite alive, and conscious, seems to do terrible things with an uncanny sense of timing. When, I ask, does a lemon *actually choose* to stall and then not start again? In front of your house on a sunny day? Of course not! You *know* that it's always at the beginning of a toll bridge, or when you're trying to sell it to someone. In the middle of a flooded street, just before the peak of a mountain road, just after you've cursed out some gorilla in the truck next to you (quick roll up the window) — a lemon is a kind of a Frankenstein monster seeking perpetual revenge for all the injustices done to it.

As for me, I have my own opinion about lemons. Though not quite like those above, it still helps to explain why they exist, how they were made, and how to recognize and avoid them. All lemons, in case you didn't know, come in three basic kinds:

(1) *The Owner Created Lemon,*
(2) *The Factory Produced Lemon, and*
(3) *The Incurable Lemon.*

The Owner (or Mechanic) Created Lemon *(lemonaris commonus)*

This species of automobile lemon is, by far, the most common, accounting for nearly 50% of all the so-called lemons. Generally speaking, most of this species are created when a lack of skill is combined with a lack of patience. The majority of these creatures are foreign-made, and suffer from negligent and/or faulty maintenance.

Perhaps the most popular example of the *Owner Created Lemon* is the common VW bug. The number of owner-caused disasters that befall these cars in particular is considerable. For instance, VW bug owners (generally) do not change their oil very frequently, which is insane considering that the feeble VW engine doesn't have an oil filter (just an oil-screen for trapping rocks). Nor do VW owners adjust the engine's valves faithfully, or tighten the belt for the cooling fan, both of which are also critical in prolonging the engine's life. These are a few of the better reasons why there are as many VW engine rebuild shops as there are McDonald's Restaurants. It isn't always the VW factory's fault when these cars go bum. (I strongly recommend John Muir's *How to Keep Your VW Bug Alive* handbook for anyone who is considering getting, or keeping, a Volkswagen.)

Another example of the mechanic-created lemon is found with Volvos, especially the pre-1975 models. For some unknown reason (perhaps because Volvos resemble U.S. built cars mechanically), people who would normally never tamper with foreign cars, bravely approach Volvos with reckless abandon. Many of these fine cars are serviced at local stations, with results that are often destructively disasterous and pitiful. No valve adjustment. Cheap parts. Totally mal-adjusted twin carburetors, and so on. I'll bet that nearly half the Volvo owners or gas station attendants in the U.S. are unaware that you cannot use regular (low octane) gasoline in the Volvo engine without drastically shortening its life!

I hope that you realize that it isn't intentional maliciousness that turns these automobiles into lemons. Very few owners or mechanics want to damage good machinery. It's often the lack of knowledge that is the true villain, and not the manufacturer. The producers of automobiles certainly make enough mistakes as it is, without being blamed for things over which they have little control.

The Factory Produced Lemon
(lemonaris assemblus incorrectus)

This category includes most cars that end up being part of a factory recall campaign. Somehow, in the production process, a basically good car gets seriously fouled-up through a temporary mistake in manufacture or design or assembly, some part of the car is built substandard and prone to early failure. Once a factory admits the error (which isn't very often), and then figures out a proper fix the car can usually be restored to reliable and safe service.

The limited-production lemon is a serious problem because (a) sometimes the factory never admits to the defect and blindly continues to build the automobiles with the same faulty part, and (b) sometimes the defect is so dangerous that you may only discover it in an unpleasant, sudden, and occasionally critical manner. Therefore, it is not a bad idea to know *which* used cars have been, at some point in their lives, the participants in a wide-based recall program.

The Incurable Lemon
(lemonaris maximus)

This type of absolute lemon is not as common as you might think. If you ponder for a moment, you'll realize that it isn't very easy to make *a whole car totally defective*. It would take a certain genius, a kind of fatal blindness, for any automobile manufacturer to achieve complete and absolute "lemon-ness". During the past fifty years of Western technology, very few car builders have actually achieved this state, in spite of some truly outstanding attempts. As luck would have it, clever engineers, mechanics and consumers have always managed to figure out a solution for the lemon's glaring defects. In the following year of production, the newer model usually appears much better behaved.

However, mankind has lately been blessed with the honor of witnessing a resurgence of the Incurable Lemon. These cars are both a rare and unusual monument to mechanical chaos and disaster, with both the U.S. and Western Europe vying for honors. I will present some of these candidates for your wonderment and admiration in a later chapter.

Cherries & Lemons

TWO

THE CASE OF THE RAVISHING RENAULT

Strong reasons make strong actions.
—William Shakespeare

It was about 4 a.m. when I finally got around to looking at the clock. My head felt like the dance floor at a tom-tom contest and the inside of my mouth tasted like the bottom of an ash tray in a pickup truck. I poured myself a couple of quick bourbons, doused my butt out in the goldfish bowl, and flipped through the fat file folder on my desk.

At age 26, Lizzie Metcalf was a beautiful and intelligent young lady. She had everything to live for, and still she had gotten mixed up in a crazy mess like this. It just doesn't add up...

O.K., now that I'm through indulging in my Mike Hammer fantasies, I really do have an interesting case in my files. Remember, if you don't read this book, this true-life case history may become your very own!

(Ominous minor chord change in background)

THE CASE OF THE RAVISHING RENAULT *(da-ram!)*

Our story begins on a bitter cold day in a small suburban community in Colorado. Lizzie Mae Metcalf, a registered nurse at the local hospital, stands impatiently at a bus stop near her home, shuffling from foot to foot, wrapping her arms about her body in a futile effort to keep warm. As usual, the bus is late again and so is Lizzie!

"This is it," she says to herself, "no more of this suffering. I'm going to buy myself a car."

Later that very same day, during her lunch break, Lizzie sits down and carefully outlines her situation. Including part of her next paycheck and all her savings, she can spend about $1,000 on a used car. She'd like to be able to shop for something a little newer than what her $1,000 will buy, but she doesn't want to enter into debt by having to pay off a big loan. Anyway, it's mostly going to be a car for driving about town, or maybe to a nearby city, so her price range is realistic enough.

Her next move is to decide what type of car she needs. Something small, easy to drive, good on snow and ice, and economical to operate and repair. Well, a VW bug sounds good. So she buys a copy of the city newspaper and starts to read the automotive ads. About halfway down a column, she spots this ad:

> **1972 RENAULT, R-16.** Very clean, low mileage, am/fm, casette tape, radials, 35 mpg, front wheel drive. Great snow car. $1,200. 555-8901 **

Lizzie has heard very little about Renaults one way or another, and the car's description is so appealing that she circles the ad and makes a mental note to call her friend Dave. He always seems to be tinkering with his car, and perhaps would offer her some good advice.

That evening, she and Dave chat for a while about her car-buying plans, and he suggests that he accompany her in order to check out the car to ensure that she buys something that isn't in need of serious repair. Although Dave doesn't know very much about Renaults, his friend Jack once owned one, and bragged about it being an economical and sporty little car.

The very next morning, Lizzie and Dave arrange to look at the car. As they pull up to the address given to them, they see a clean, shiny, and extremely attractive maroon Renault parked in front of the house. After the initial formalities, everyone goes for a test ride and Lizzie is certainly impressed with the car's comfort and agility. This car beats a VW hands down, she thinks, although it does seem a bit under-powered climbing hills.

"Oh, it just needs a good tune up," says the owner.

(Enter the Violin Section)

The owner seems like quite a nice person, and Dave gives his stamp of approval. Within several minutes the deal is closed for the reduced price of $1,000 and Lizzie makes arrangements to return to pick up her new acquisition the following Monday morning.

When Lizzie visits the Motor Vehicle Office to register her new car, she discovers that she owes a 6% Sales Tax ($60.00), a Title Transfer Fee ($3.00), and the next year's Plate Fee ($22.00). In addition, she learns that the Renault was not registered for the entire year before, (how peculiar!), and this makes the new registrant liable for the past due unpaid tax. According to the Law, it must be paid by *someone*, regardless of whether the car is actually registered yearly or not. This was an additional fee of $20.00, afterwhich she trekked into the insurance office to pay her first installment ($70.00), on the basic no-fault liability insurance policy. All of these extra costs ($175.00 in total), take her by surprise, so she calls her parents and borrows what she needs.

On Tuesday, she drops the car off at the neighborhood service station for the necessary tune-up, where they remind her of the required annual State Inspection due before the end of the month as well. Since it only costs $5.00, she tells the mechanic to do that also.

That evening, after work, she returns to the station and finds to dismay that: (a) her Renault doesn't need a "tune-up", but rather a complete valve job (low compression), and (b) her car fails the State Inspection due to worn-out rear brakes, a broken light lens and some minor electrical work to make the horn operate.

"Good Grief! How much will this cost?" she inquires.

"Well, providing that we can get all the parts, the whole shot will come to about $200 or $250," replies the mechanic, whirling a toothpick in his left ear.

"Well, I guess I have little choice," she laments sadly, "but why should parts be a problem to get? I remember checking to see if there was a Renault dealer in town, and there certainly is!"

"Yup, that's right," he replies, "but *your car* hasn't been built for over five years now. Kinda *obsolete model*, you might say, and dealers in smaller towns just don't stock many of the parts for these older cars. They got all the money tied-up in parts for the new Renaults."

Lizzie is, to use a familiar phrase, totally bummed-out. Yet, she courageously decides that the *only way from here is up!* The following day she arranges for a loan through her Hospital Credit Union. She borrows $300, just in case something else comes up. As it turns out, she proves to be very intuitive!

After six weeks of waiting for parts, Lizzie's car is again ready to roll, with a bill of $346.83 attached to the windshield. It happens that the brake drums were far too damaged to be of use anymore, and new ones cost quite a bit. Then too, there was the leaking brake cylinder that needed replacement, along with a new fuel filter, some antifreeze, a new fan belt and wiper blades. You know, the usual stuff.

So, the first mile on Lizzie's freshly purchased used car cost exactly $1,521.82. You would think that after all this, Lizzie would live happily forever after. But not quite.

She was happy all right, at least for a few days, until she accidently hit one of the pot holes that speckle the winter roads in Colorado's snow country. She had been driving at a very reasonable speed, enjoying the scenery and feeling quite pleased about how well her car was running, when she suddenly hit the hole. Some fifty yards later, she heard a snapping sound, and within a few brief moments, she became distinctly aware that the car was tilting towards the rider's side.

She wasn't sure what had happened, but just to play it safe, she quite wisely had the car towed back to town ($35) to the neighborhood garage. The mechanic promptly checked it out and found that Lizzie's car had a broken torsion bar in the Renault's rather peculiar suspension system. Furthermore, the garage admitted knowing very little about fixing this specific problem, and suggested that she have it towed to the authorized dealer's service department.

After another tow, $15 later, a quick examination revealed that it was indeed the torsion bar, broken from the impact with the pot hole. Lizzie was told that a new one would have to be special-ordered from the East Coast, or perhaps directly from France and this would have to be *paid for in advance.* So, Lizzie shelled over the $66...and waited.

She waited and she waited, and the wind roared and the snow blew and the bus stops were not fit for man or beast. But nurses without cars had little choice.

A month later, the part did arrive and Lizzie was again back on the highways, after an additional $50 installation fee. The total cost of her unfortunate meeting with an ordinary pothole? $156.00. Thus far, the car has cost Lizzie a total of $1,677.82 for which she has driven a mere 112 miles.

When the trip odometer turned 325 miles, a short two weeks later, a tire on the Renault went flat while parked in the hospital lot.

Attempting to change it, Lizzie found that her spare was also flat. With a friend, she took one tire to a nearby gas station. There she learned that the tire rim would not fit on most common tire-repair machines. You see, it's like this: a special adapter is required for working on rims of French cars. Since there are so few of these cars in the area, most service stations do not bother to buy the tool. However, the authorized Renault dealer will certainly have the proper adapter.

Then off to the dealer, who of course, was not open on Saturdays. Lizzie's car sat for the weekend in a parking lot at the hospital, where overnight parking was not permitted. So, she went off to the police station to explain her plight.

By the time Lizzie returned home, she was disgusted, a defeated and beaten woman. *She wanted out –O–U–T–––and right now!* After several days, her ad appeared in the local newspapers, on laundromat bulletin boards, and most appropriately, in the rear window of her beautiful, but cruel Renault R-16.

To make this long story somewhat shorter, it wasn't easy to sell the car, and after three weeks of ads ($15), and not without some guilt feelings about selling it to the new owner, Lizzie managed to sell her car for $900. Consequently, in the period of three months, she has driven the Renault just over 300 miles and completely lost about $800. A full year's savings gone with none of the compensations one might have gotten from loss by fire or flood. For all that money spent, she didn't even have a good time!

I could easily re-tell many similar "up-beat" stories, but I'm sure that most people have already heard them, ones like them, or even worse! However, there is a great deal to be learned from Lizzie's sad tale. Consider, for a moment, the unfortunate mistakes that she made:

(1) *She was improperly prepared to deal with the hidden costs involved in the purchase of a used car.*

(2) *She bought a used car that was over-priced, obsolete, difficult to find parts for, and awkward to repair.*

(3) *She consulted a friend who was in no way qualified to offer her accurate advice.*

(4) *She did not have the car checked over by a good garage or diagnostic center.*

(5) *She allowed her eyes and instincts to over-rule her sense of practicality.*

That last point, (5), is often criticized for being harsh, since it is *only human* to appreciate things beyond their function; to which I can only reply; that in the matters of buying a good used car, we are not talking about romance, adventure, or lofty ideals, which are also human things as well! We are simply addressing ourselves to the task of buying a car, a metal capsule or box on wheels that burns gasoline, and there is no advantage in getting romantic about something like that, right?

The entire central theme of this book is to make certain that *you* don't have an experience similar to Lizzie's. Yet, misfortunes like hers happen to unsuspecting car buyers every day. Luckily for you, everything you need to know to keep away from one of these soap-opera melodramas is coming up in the following chapters, where you will learn about the *very best* and the *very worst* cars you could choose to buy.

THREE

THE BEST AND THE WORST

The total number of cars registered in the U.S. is about 114 million. Of these, 17% are less than two years old, and 70% are between two and ten years old. Only 13% survive beyond ten years. On the average, automobiles end in the junkpile after 6.2 years.

Many used car guides are far too lenient and understanding of the obvious failures created by the auto industry, and from a mechanic's point of view this leads to unnecessary hassles for the average consumer. Buying manuals have a tendency to tactfully de-emphasize major problems and praise things of little importance. For instance, to say that the Ford Pinto has *"fuel system difficulties"* is an awfully nice way to mention that this car may burst into a vehicular Molitov Cocktail when rear-ended, giving passengers no chance for escape. Likewise, to recommend a Fiat over a Datsun simply because of *"considerably more legroom"* is a great disservice to all car buyers, except those who may enjoy kicking themselves.

I have no intention of being overly kind to the lemons of the automobile world and will avoid yet another pitfall of many other used car buying guides, namely a ponderous amount of detailed information that would take the reader countless hours of study. Of course, it may be a fine idea to publish each and every Factory Recall Campaign that has ever been launched, but not in this chapter. It is safe to assume that by the time you get your hands on a used car the factory defects have been corrected by previous owners, or may simply never show up on your car at all. Unfortunately, if you have ideas of finding a car which has *never* been subject to a factory recall, you will have very little choice. Every automobile manufacturer is plagued by them and even the most popular makes, like VW, have a high number of recalls against them. Essentially, I intend to mention *only* the very best and very worst used cars that are available today, steering you away from the disasters and leading you to the shining stars of Detroit, Europe, and Japan.

The recommendations in this chapter are not based upon government reports or bribe-soaked consumer evaluations, but rather originate from the real world experiences of car owners and car fixers. It is the owners and mechanics who are the *real* experts. These are the people who deal with the actual day to day hassles and pleasures of all automobiles. After the warranties have expired; after all the car magazines and consumer publications have returned their road test samples; and after the razzle dazzle advertising hype disappears- - - the car becomes but one of other millions belonging to some person who then must deal with it in the real working world. *We* are the people that discover, often the hard way, some of the most unbearable and poorly engineered cars ever made - - these same cars that were once lauded highly and recommended by automotive experts and consumer groups. Only the test of time can reveal the awful truth about some automobiles, but not until countless hundreds of thousands of new and used car owners suffer the consequences of having been deceived and misled.

Using the experiences of car owners and mechanics to define good and bad cars seems to me a practical and sound approach. If, for instance, 49 out of 50 people express to me that Car X stinks, then there may well be something to it. No matter what the product's defenders might say, that car should be looked on suspiciously. Who would know better than the people who drive and repair these cars? Cars, as we all know, like race horses, prize fighters, politicians, wines and local bars, develop an undeniable reputation; a performance pattern who relation with their owners eventually generate *"the word"*. Lies have short legs, and die out, but the truth sticks. The writing is on countless repair shop walls and checkbook stubs. To read the writing, all one has to do is clear the air of advertising myths and personal prejudices. Blind product loyalty is not a safe course of action, especially today!

I urge you to carefully read this entire chapter prior to making any decision about the kind of car you might want to buy. For convenience, I have divided the chapter into two major sections, one for American cars and the other for Imported makes. Also, there is a brief section on trucks and vans and some quick notes on motorcycles and mopeds.

American Cars

Through the past eighty years thousands of different car models have been manufactured in the United States. Most companies were completely wiped-out during the Great Depression, while those that survived were consumed by predatory corporate actions of the 1950's. Today, **General Motors** remains most powerful; constantly on guard against forcing its remaining competitors, **Ford** and **Chrysler,** out of business. Aside from these "Big Three" manufacturers, only **American Motors** and the limited production **Checker Motors Corporation** remain.

A popular myth created by mass-advertising is that America produces inferior quality cars when compared to imports. Although it may be true that U.S. cars are often less carefully assembled, more wasteful on gas, clumsy on the road, and dull to drive, none of these detractions mean that they are less reliable or poorly engineered.

The snobbery against American cars is a social game amongst elitist car owners, but from the vantage point of the mechanic, who works on all kinds of cars, nothing is further from the truth. No car in the world can take sheer abuse like an American car can. With low compression, burned spark plugs, and a crank case filled with sludge, (once known as oil) most U.S. cars still refuse to quit. In comparison, European cars are temperamental, high strung, and demand more maintenance and expense for day-to-day reliable service.

Foreign car owners may boast about their incredible mileage, but rarely tell you that the 100,000 or 150,000 mile mark was reached only after enormous expense and with the application of meticulous care. Meanwhile, most American cars rarely see the business end of a garden hose or a clean rag, while in countries like Switzerland a car with even a dented fender is so rare that they are placed into museums for the very young to wonder at.

American engineering is good enough for the likes of Rolls Royce, Ferrari and Jaguar; which use the GM400ZA Turbo Hydramatic transmission. Volvo uses a slightly altered version of a Borg Warner unit often found in American Motors cars. In fact the mileage logged by the average Greyhound Bus would put the finest cars in Europe to shame.

Of course, *the best foreign cars are still far superior to the worst American autos,* and this may account for why so many imports are popular today. Keep in mind, however, that for a very modest sum, certain American cars will deliver thousands of miles of trouble-free service. Even if these U.S. built cars may cost more to feed, they are still among the very best machines in the world for getting you from place to place without hassle.

For your convenience, American cars are grouped by corporations so you may know who builds what model. In this way, you can be more selective, just in case you may want to boycott some company that fired your grandad forty years ago, or exercise some other personal gripe.

Finally, you'll notice that I am somewhat prejudiced against the bigger gas slurping cars. The reason for this is that I live in a large crowded city where big cars are very impractical. I'm sure that larger cars may make more sense in the country, or perhaps with a large family. Hopefully, by explaining my bias for small cars, I will remind you to think carefully about the size of car you really need.

Explanation Of The Rating System

Both American and Foreign automobiles are rated on a scale of EXCELLENT, GOOD, AVERAGE and FAIR.

EXCELLENT means that the cars listed have established a reputation for reliability and have the desired qualities of reasonable size and economy. Cars in this group hold a higher average resale value and are a good investment for the used car buyer.

GOOD means that the cars listed are *basically reliable*, but because of their initial price, maintenance cost, size, lack of economy, or restriction to unleaded gas, these automobiles cannot be the most desireable to own.

AVERAGE means that the cars listed are *not bad enough to be outright lemons*, but show little merit. There cars will run o.k., but they are often a nuisance to own, and in many cases offer the owner nothing in terms of comfort, ease of repair and quality. If these cars were sandwiches, the bread would be dry, the lettuce limp, the meat stale, but they wouldn't actually poison you.

POOR *is an outright warning!* May all of these cars be melted down, reforged, or buried, lest their metal return to contaminate other cars! Do not, under any circumstances, buy any car that is rated this way.

The General Motors Corporation

First formed in 1908 by W. C. Durant, this massive industrial complex builds Buick, Cadillac, Chevrolet, Oldsmobile and Pontiac. It also manufactures GMC Trucks and Buses. Today this single corporation dominates the American automotive industry, setting all trends for design and price that all other manufacturers loyally adhere to.

Oldsmobile

Historically, the *Oldsmobile* is the oldest surviving automobile make in the United States, now some 85 years on the road. This car has always been the technological leader among the General Motors line, offering an automatic transmission to the public in 1938, the first overhead valve V-8 (in normal production) engine in 1949, front wheel drive in 1966 and a deisel engine in 1978. Since the 1950's, when Oldsmobiles were regarded as large "prestige cars" below the Cadillac on the socio-economic ladder, this branch of General Motors has diversified greatly.

The first Oldsmobile compact, the *F-85 Cutlass*, was introduced in 1961, and after several years of ironing-out the bugs, it became a successful and popular automobile. In 1973, to help balance the growing chasm between its larger and smaller models, Oldsmobile introduced the *Omega*, a slightly altered version of the Buick Apollo. The *Omega* filled the intermediate spot in the Oldsmobile line, and then in 1975 the *Starfire* completed its compact category. Here again, the *Starfire* is the Oldsmobile hybrid version of the Buick Skylark, the Chevrolet

Monza, and the Pontiac Sunbird. Of course, Oldsmobile is still manufacturing their version of the standard Detroit tank, the prestigious *Ninety-Eight* series, as well as the somewhat smaller *Cutlass* series.

Today, Oldsmobile is manufacturing and marketing America's first full production deisel car to compete with the imported models of Mercedes, Peugeot and the VW Rabbit. It recently introduced a new series of front-wheel-drive compacts for the 1980's to replace its present compacts, hopefully to give the public a more tempting alternative to the expanded import market.

Buicks

The first Buicks appeared in 1903 and have since enjoyed great popularity. Similar to the Oldsmobile, General Motors has directed the once massive Buick "tank image" towards a more appealing family-car line. In 1961 Buick introduced its first compact, the *Special-Skylark* series. Over the years this model has been well received, but curiously by 1969 it had evolved to a nearly full-size car to join the other models in the Buick line.

In 1973, Buick again set its aim by introducing the *Apollo* series, this time as "an intermediate size car" made to appeal to those drivers who wanted something between a compact and a house on wheels. Buick's version of the General Motors compact series is the *Skyhawk*, first introduced in 1975. This model like Oldsmobile's is being marketed as the front-wheel-drive compact for the 1980's. Also like Oldsmobile, Buick manufactures a full range of large motor vehicles such as the *LeSabre*, the *Electra*, and the *Riviera*. These are powerful, big, strong, reliable cars that appeal to the determined big-car enthusiast.

Cadillac

Henry M. Leland, the founder of the Cadillac, was a perfectionist as an engineer, and his personal influence created the reputation for Cadillac's outstanding quality. Only several years ago, the Cadillac was still considered as "The Standard of the World", but with rising fuel prices and more stringent emmission standards, few can deny that our world has seriously changed, and that these cars fail to fit in as well as they once did.

Large, full-sized Cadillacs, such as the *DeVille* and *Fleetwood* series, are still the bread-and-butter models according to Cadillac spokesmen, even though the company has begun taking a more realistic approach to size with its smaller *Seville* model which represents nearly 25% of its present sales and is available with a deisel engine. It seems that the executive board of Cadillac is beginning to understand, as Europeans have long known, that a car need not be utterly monstrous in order to be safe, stable and luxurious. Finally, many people still look at the Cadillac as a somewhat vulgar display of wealth, but I fail to understand why *this* car shoud be singled out, with so many other vulgar American cars to choose from.

Chevrolet

The Chevrolet line has always been one of my favorites, ever since its outstanding 1955 model which benchmarked an important design stage in the exterior modernization of all American automobiles. As the Fifties progressed, if you believe that to be progress, the Chevrolet grew bigger and bigger until it was nearly 210 inches in length in 1962. Unfortunately, this was a nice size for a Ponderosa Pine but a bit ridiculous for a passenger car. Chevrolet finally accepted hints from Ford and Chrysler and developed a fine compact car in 1962, introduced then as the *Chevy II*. The practical-sized, successful *CheryII* was built up until 1968, when it merged into Chevrolet's *Nova* and *Chevelle* series, and represented a bigger "intermediate" automobile line. In 1971 Chevrolet entered into the sub-compact market with a modestly priced *Vega* series designed to compete with Ford's Pinto and various Japanese and European imports. It had been expected that the *Vega* would be both favorably accepted and more popular than Chevrolet's earlier, ill-fated *Corvair* models (1960-1969) which were plagued by some serious design failures. However, instead of living up to such lofty goals, the *Vega* became one of Chevrolet's greatest disappointments and became quickly replaced in 1975 by the Chevy *Monza*. By taking a place alongside the other General Motors' challengers to imports, the *Monza* was Chevrolets' version of the *Skyhawk* and *Starfire*. (The new front-wheel drive *Citation* is a further extension of this unified GM approach). Meanwhile, the *Nova* and the *Camero* (1967) have evolved to become Chevrolet's intermediate and sports sedan line.

In 1976 Chevrolet introduced the sub-compact little *Chevette* to directly compete with the ever rising import of mini-cars from Europe and Japan. The *Chevette's* design was inspired by General Motor's European ally, Opel of Germany. Currently, the *Caprice* and *Monte Carlo* represent the Chevrolet big car line, while the ever-popular *Corvette* still remains strong, although with much less muscle than it once enjoyed.

Pontiac

The *Pontiac* was first conceived as a lower priced running mate to the Oakland in 1926. At that time both cars were being manufactured by the Oakland Motor company which was consumed by General Motors in 1933. During the next 30 years, Pontiac worked at producing a conservative large-bodied automobile, competing mostly with Plymouth, Mercury and other sedate makes.

In 1961 Pontiac made its first entry into the compact market with an extremely bizarre *Tempest* model. This uniquely designed automobile used a large four-cylinder engine to drive a rear-mounted transmission, via a thin flexible cable. A closer examination in 1964 led to a normalized version of the *Tempest*, which sold well as a reasonable American compact until 1971, when it melted into the *LeMans* series. In 1967 Pontiac released its *Firebird* model as a competitor to the very popular Ford Mustang and Chevrolet Camero in the sports sedan category. In 1975, Pontiac's version of the Vega appeared, called the *Astra*, which was quickly phased-out in favor of the 1976-77 beginnings of the *Sunbird*. This compact-like car is nearly identical to the Chevrolet Monza, the Buick Skylark, and the Oldsmobile Starfire. Each of these vary only slightly in having different overcoats. The Pontiac version of an "intermediate car" is the *Ventura*, amazingly similar in many respects to the Buick Apollo and the Oldsmobile Omega. Rounding out the heavy metal class are Pontiac's larger full-size vehicles, the *Bonneville* and the *Grand Prix*.

Ratings For General Motors Cars

EXCELLENT

Oldsmobile F-85/Cutlass	1964-1972
Buick Special/Skylark	1964-1969
Chevrolet, Full Size	1955-1956
Chevy II	1964-1968
Chevrolet Nova	1968-1971
Chevrolet Camero	1967-1971
Chevelle	All Years to 1971
Malibu	All Years to 1971
Corvette	All Years to 1967

GOOD

Chevrolet, Full Size	All Years (*)
Chevelle	1972 on up
Chevy Malibu	1972 on up
Corvette	1968 on up
Chevrolet Camaro	1972 on up
Chevrolet Nova	1972 on up
Buick Skylark	1970-1972
Buick, Full Size	All Years (*)
Oldsmobile, Full Size	All Years
Cadillac	All Years
Pontiac Tempest	1964-1971 (*)
Pontiac Firebird	All Years (6 cyl)

(*) See POOR Category for exceptions.

AVERAGE

Chevrolet Monza	1976 on up (V-8 +)
Chevette	1977 on up
Buick Apollo	1974-1975 (8 cyl +)
Buick Skyhawk	1975 on up
Oldsmobile Omega	1973 on up
Oldsmobile Starfire	1975 on up
Oldsmobile Toronado	All Years
Pontiac Ventura	1972 on up
Pontiac LeMans	All Years
Pontiac Sunbird	1976 on up (6 cyl +)

POOR

Chevy Corvair	All Years
Chevy Vega	All Years
Chevrolet, Full Size	1957-1961 w. Turboglide
Buick Special	1961-1963
Buick Skylark	1961-1963
Oldsmobile F-85	1961-1963
Oldsmobile Cutlass	1961-1963
Pontiac Astre	All Years
Pontiac Tempest	1966-1968 w. o.h. cam 6

(NOTE: Buick Opel listed under "German Cars")

The Ford Motor Company

Henry Ford built his first car in 1896 and sold his first production auto in 1903. In 1909 he introduced the world famous Model T which revolutionized and put the world on wheels for better or worse. The Father of the modern assembly line built and sold 15 million Model T's in 18 years, which in 1925 sold for only $260.

The Ford Motor Company is today a worldwide manufacturing giant with subsidiary companies in England, Germany, Canada and who knows where else. Among its products are the Ford, Mercury and Lincoln automobiles, as well as Ford Trucks and farm equipment. It is today, one of the last remaining family owned giant corporations in the world.

Ford

The Ford motor car was the most popular automobile in the United States until the 1930's, when Henry Ford's reluctance to modernize his cars allowed Chevrolet to gain in sales advantage. The trend for yearly model style changes was then established by General Motors, and since then, Ford Motors has been playing catch-up, often just following the successful leads of its chief competitor. Surprisingly however, Ford occasionally outguesses General Motors, as for example, in 1960 when it first introduced the compact *Falcon* series, beating Chevrolet to the punch by several years. This was a simple compact with a 6 cylinder engine, and as the years went by it became fancier and stylistically more attractive. Ford's second coup was its advanced introduction of the sport sedan

Mustang series in 1964. This car has been one of the most successful sellers in modern automotive history. Over one-half million sold in 18 months isn't bad.

In 1969 Ford began to diversify even further in small cars, coming out with the *Maverick*, a bare-bones compact to fit under the grown-up bigger Falcon. The 1970's unfortunately have brought far less good fortune to Ford. In 1970, Ford introduced its sub-compact *Pinto* which originally sold quite well, giving buyers a choice of a German Ford or (less desireable) English Ford powertrain. Since its introduction the *Pinto* has received much bad publicity and legal problems owing to its poorly designed fuel-tank placement. The intermediate and large car lines have also been plagued by numerous factory recall campaigns. Consequently, the 1978 European-sized *Fairmont* represents Ford's serious attempt to regain public confidence in its vehicles.

Mercury

The first Mercury was manufactured by Ford in 1939. Its image has always been very conservative, geared to those buyers who fit in between lower-priced Ford owners and the higher-priced Lincoln owners. The Mercury line resembles the Ford models very closely; the early *Comet* series matches the Falcon, but perhaps less attractive; later Mercury *Comets* of 1971 imitate the Ford Maverick line; the Mercury *Cougar* is a close cousin to the Mustang; and the Mercury *Bobcat* has the identical bad habits of the nearly identical Ford Pinto.

In the late 1970's, Mercury introduces its version of the Ford Granada under the banner of the *Mon-*

arch, and the even newer Mercury model *Zephyr* closely resembles the Ford Fairmont. The Mercury *Capri* is a near twin to the Ford Mustang, and is listed under German cars in the foreign section.

Lincoln

Lincoln became part of the Ford automobile empire in 1922 and has always been large and powerful. They were the favorite cars of gangsters during prohibition, capable of speeds well over 80 mph way back in the roaring 20's. President Coolidge bought one, which may have been one of the best things he ever did, as far as history can judge. Lincolns have been at the White House ever since. There's even a Lincoln parked at the Kremlin, and as far as I know, there haven't been any complaints. Without a doubt, Lincoln has built some magnificent cars throughout the years. In 1977 Lincoln produced its answer to the Cadillac Seville with its *Versailles* model which is based on the Ford Granada body.

Ratings For Ford Motors Cars

EXCELLENT
Ford Falcon............... 1964-1970
Ford Fairlane............. 1964-1970
Ford Mustang............. 1964-1966

GOOD
Ford Mustang............. 1967-1970
Lincolns .... All Years

AVERAGE
Ford Mustangs .... 1971 on up
Ford, Full Size .... All Years
Mustang II .... All Years
Maverick .... All Years
Ford Granada.............. All Years
Mercury Comet............. All Years
Mercury Cougar .... All Years
Mercury Monarch .... 1975 on up
Mercury, Full Size........... All Years

POOR
Ford Pinto................ All Years
Mercury Bobcat .... All Years

(IN ALL CATEGORIES REGULAR GASOLINE PREFERRED)

NOTE: The Mercury Zephyr, like the Ford Fairmont is too new to rate.

The Chrysler Corporation

Chrysler was the last of the Big Three automobile manufacturers to arrive in the Detroit-scene. It was formed in 1928 and was comprised of Chrysler, Dodge, and Plymouth.

In 1961 the DeSoto line was ended, and the remaining three models diversified, with Chrysler producing only large V-8 cars while Dodge and Plymouth competed with other models on the intermediate and compact level. The popular compact Plymouth *Valiant,* created in 1960, and its companion Dodge *Dart*, started in 1963, have been the two most successful cars ever produced by the Chrysler Corporation. At the present time, Chrysler has sold much of its overseas interests in Europe and has begun channeling this capital into developing newer and smaller cars for the domestic market, such as the front-wheel drive *Omni* and *Horizon.*

Chrysler

With the exception of a brief tail-fin era during the 1950's, Chryslers have been jumbo sized. So, anyone interested in an economy car will not find it here. However, the early and mid-60's Chryslers with the 383 V-8 are amazingly strong and reliable, and somewhat easier to push about than a comparably big Cadillac, Buick or Oldsmobile.

Dodge

One of the most popular compact cars ever made in America has been the Dodge *Dart* series. Previous to this model, Dodge had the compact *Lancer*, which was actually a Plymouth *Valiant* in disguise, but was dropped in favor of the shrinking *Dart* in 1963. These compacts were technically interesting at the time, with torsion bar suspension instead of coil springs, alternator ignition, and a fine slant-six (inclined to one side) engine of excellent power and durability. Along with these cars, Dodge also has developed a full line of Detroit combat tanks, such as the *Coronet, Charger, Challenger, Polara,* and *Monaco,* all big strong cars that as a rule seem to handle better than their General Motors and Ford counterparts. The Dodge *Colt* appears under the Foreign Car Section.

Plymouth

The modern Plymouth parallels the Dodge quite closely through the 60's and 70's. Plymouth's compact, called the *Valiant*, first appeared on the roads in 1960. A sort of compact sport coupe was added in 1964 and was called the *Barracuda*. Meanwhile, in the heavy cruiser class, Plymouth produced the *Belvedere, Road Runner* and *Satellite*, and in the battleship fleet the *Fury, Fury III* and the *Sport Fury*.

Chrysler Corporation Ratings

EXCELLENT

Dodge Dart . . . . 1963 on up, 6 cyl better
Dodge Swinger . . . . 1969 on up, "225" better
Dodge Demon. . . . . 1971 on up,
Dodge Custom . . . . All Years
Plymouth Valiant . . . . All Years 6 cyl. better
Plymouth Scamp. . . . . All Years "225" better
Plymouth Duster. . . . . All Years

GOOD

Chrysler, Full Size. . . . . to 1966
Dodge, Full Size . . . . to 1966
Plymouth, Full Size. . . . . to 1966
Plymouth, Volare . . . . 1977 on up is better
Dodge Aspen . . . . 1977 on up is better

AVERAGE

Chrysler, Full Size. . . . . 1967 on up
Plymouth, Full Size. . . . . 1967 on up
Dodge, Full Size . . . . 1967 on up
Dodge Aspen 1976
Plymouth Barracuda . . . . 1967-1969 6 cyl. better

POOR

Plymouth Barracuda . . . . 1970 on up

NOTE: The Dodge Omni and Plymouth Horizon are too new to rate (comments are mixed). The Dodge Colt and Plymouth Arrow are listed under Japanese Cars, and the Plymouth Cricket appears under English Cars. The new Dodge Challenger and the Plymouth Sapporo, also from Japan, are too new to rate, but the Japanese manufacturer has a good reputation.

The American Motors Corporation

This automobile manufacturer was founded in 1954 after the merger of two very sick companies, Nash Motors and Hudson Motors. The apparent result was the present single very sick company. In 1958, American Motors dropped all other model names except "Rambler" and built a complete series of very uninspired vehicles distinguishable only by little American flag decals in the rear window. This rather uninventive period lasted about ten years, after which American Motors Corporation again came to life in 1968 with some attractive, modern autos, like the *Javelin* and the *AMX* Sport Coupes, both in the Ford Mustang tradition. In 1969 and 1970, the compact *Hornet* series and its sawed-off cousin, the *Gremlin*, were introduced.

In 1970, AMC merged with Jeep, a move that probably saved the company. In 1975, the visually unique *Pacer* appeared as AMC's attempt to diversify even further. The most recent compact is the *Spirit*, this company's answer to the *Chevette*.

Ratings

EXCELLENT and GOOD
(None)

AVERAGE
AMC Javelin/AMX. 1967-74
AMC Hornet. . . . . All Years
AMC Matador. . . . . All Years
AMC Ambassador . . . . 1967 on up

POOR
AMC Gremlin. . . . . All Years
AMC Pacer. All Years
Rambler . . . . All Years
AMC Ambassador . . . . to 1966

(NOTE: AMC Jeep appears in section on Trucks)

The Studebaker-Packard Corporation

The last true Packard was built in 1956, while the final Studebaker appeared in 1966. Both of these cars were good in their days, but neither would be a practical automobile for the average car owner of the 1980's.

Probably the only Studebaker you will find available is the *Lark* series; good strong cars of reasonable size. They were made from 1959-1966 and most parts are still available (except things like trim, lenses and glass). Be careful to buy one that is relatively intact. A stick shift six would be ok, although I think the V-8 is stronger.

Checker Motors Corporation

Checker has been building taxicabs for many years but are newcomers to the passenger car market, first making their cars available to the public in the late 50's. These cars are legendary for their toughness and incredible roominess, as well as being virtually indestructable. It is not uncommon to hear these cars going over 200,000 miles without a major engine overhaul, and some claims reach the half-million mile distance!

In spite of the good things, Checkers are rather unpleasant cars to drive, and are not recommended for the average car owner. *Under no condition should you buy a used Checker cab.* Once the cab company sells them, they are very tired automobiles.

Foreign Cars

Foreign automobiles had very little impact in the United States until the mid-50's when Volkswagen began the mass exportation of its popular VW "Bug." Prior to that, most foreign cars were considered to be expensive and thrilling toys that broke down all the time.

The secret of VW's tremendous popularity was undoubtedly the old story of "the right product for the right time." By today's standards, the early VW, absent even of a fuel gauge seems a quite drab and primitive vehicle, yet back then it was fun, reasonably reliable, and very cheap to run. Compared to the colossal American cars of the time, the VW Bug was indeed a treat.

By the early 1960's, an active marketing battle had developed between Volkswagen, Renault, the English cars and some of the new American compacts. Within a few years, it became more and more obvious that VW and the Americans had won because of their better products.

In 1968, the Japanese created drastic changes in the American import car market by blowing their competition off the map with a series of excellent and economical cars.

Throughout the 1970's, the situation remained much the same with Japan on top of the import market and Germany making a solid comeback, while the French, Italians, and Swedes continued thinking of new ways to regain what had been lost. The English could only compete on a very minor scale.

Foreign built cars in this section are grouped by their country, primarily because I find that many people are confused when it comes to figuring out which car comes from what part of the world.

England

The English build several makes of automobiles, some of them being *Austin, Jaguar, M.G., Triumph, Sunbeam, Hillman and Rolls Royce.* There are others that come to mind, but many if not all have gone out of business in the past decade.

Without a doubt, the British automobile and motorcycle industries have been in grave danger of collapse for many years. They have been unable to put together a competitive product, are overcome by labor problems, and have failed to develop a viable overseas network of dealers. Consequently, with such severe pressure from Europe and Japan, the British have lost the ability to capture either the interest or the dollar of car buyers outside their island Commonwealth.

English cars, nonetheless, can be very beautiful. English cars can be fun to drive. English cars can also be an incredible nuisance.

I'm certain that back home it's better, with plenty of competent interested mechanics who are used to working on their own country's cars and on automobiles not equipped with complex emission control devices. But not in the United States — the last thing you would want is an English built used car.

Regrettably, I cannot recommend *any* English auto for you. This includes the *Plymouth Cricket.*

NO RECOMMENDATIONS

France

French automobiles have always been a great mystery to me and the most difficult for me to comprehend. This confusion may well be partly cultural, for I am convinced that a 1955 Chevy must likewise appear confusing to a French mechanic. Yet, French engineering, that is, the methods they use to solve a mechanical problem, seems unduly complex to me, both in theory and execution. Why is it so hard to repair *anything* in a French built auto? Why can't parts be made available to repair French built cars? Why do so many American mechanics shudder and cringe at the mere sight of a French built automobile?

Well, I don't know the answers to these questions, but the reality of the situation is that a used French car in the U.S. can be a giant hassle because of the scarcity of parts and near absence of service. As pretty and competent as *Renaults, Simcas, Peugeots* and *Citroens* may be, trying to cope with one in this country is difficult.

RATING OF FRENCH CARS

EXCELLENT and GOOD
(None)

AVERAGE
Peugeot 403, 404, 304 . . . . All Years (*)
Renault, R5 (Le Car) . . . . All Years (*)
(*) Standard transmission only.

POOR
Simca . . . . All Years
Citroen . . . . All Years
Peugeot, 504 . . . . All Years
Renault, R8, 10, 12-17 . . . . All Years
Renault, 4CV . . . . All Years
Renault, Caravelle . . . . All Years
Renault, Dauphine . . . . All Years

Germany

Americans have often felt that the best foreign cars are built in Germany. With the current deluge of excellent Japanese automobiles being offered, this long-standing view may today be in dispute, but it is still undeniable that makes such as *Mercedes-Benz, BMW, Porshe, Volkswagen, Audi, Capri* and *Opel* offer a standard of automotive quality to the world.

RATING OF GERMAN CARS

EXCELLENT

Mercedes-Benz 220 Sb . . . . 1959-67 (*)
Mercedes-Benz 220 SEB . . . . .1959-67 (*)

(*) Standard shift only.

GOOD

BMW, 2002 1973-75
BMW, 530 i . . . . 1976 on up (*)
BMW, 320 i . . . . 1977 on up (*)
Capri. . . . . 1972 on up
VW, Bug/Ghia. 1963-1973
Opel, Manta 1973-75
Porsche, 356. . . . . All Years
Mercedes-Benz . . . . All Years   (**)
Ford, Fiesta . . . . All Years

(*) Standard shift preferred
(**) See exception in Poor category

AVERAGE

BMW 2002. . . . . .All Years to 1972
BMW 530 i. . . . . 1975 only
BMW 3.0S, Si, CS, CSA . . . . All Years
Capri. 1970-71
VW Bug. . . . . 1974 on up
VW Super Beetle. . . . . All Years
VW Dasher. . . . . 1975 on up
VW Rabbit. . . . . 1976 on up
VW Scirocco. . . . . All Years
Opel . . . . All Years (**)
Porshe. . . . . All Years

(*) See exception in Poor category.   POOR

POOR

Audi	All Years
BMW, Bavaria	All Years
VW Thing	All Years
VW Fastback,	All Years
VW Squareback	All Years
VW 411, 412	All Years
VW Rabbit	1975 only
VW Dasher	1974 only
VW Van/Pickup, all models	All Years
Opel GT	All Years
Mercedes-Benz 600	All Years

Italy

Italian cars suffer in the United States market from the same problems that plague the British and the French auto manufacturers — few parts, few dealers, and no luck. Their cars just do not perform as well here, partially due to the emission devices that are required in the U.S., and partially due to curious designs that are yet to be explored by most Americans.

All in all, *Fiat* owners complain the most, and while they claim to enjoy driving their cars, most seem very anxious never to repeat the mistake of buying one again. I agree with them. Who wants a car like the *128*, when you have to nearly cut the front end of it off with an acetylene torch to replace a set of ignition points?

Owners of the Alfa-Romeo automobiles seem to tolerate their cars more, but I never have met one who has not spent beaucoup bucks on their little Italian hummers.

Italian cars are enjoyable to drive and economical on gas, but alas, they cannot stay out of the repair shop. You might take a worthwhile tip from the old slogan of the extinct Packard Motor Company: *"Ask the man who owns one."*

NO RECOMMENDATIONS

Japan

In 1968 Japan imported the **Datsun 510** and a new version of the **Toyota Corona** to the United States and struck terror in the hearts and minds of American and European automakers. They are still trying to catch up with the Japanese more than 10 years later, but Honda, Toyota and Subaru are running away with the import market and will likely continue through the early 1980's.

The reason behind the great success of the Japanese cars is simple — when compared to the competition, they give a car buyer the most for the money. So what if you can't impress people with one? They run cheaply, don't break down very often, and if given proper care, can reach 100,000 miles without a major overhaul. They are also the leaders in emission control technology which isn't a bad talent to have these days.

RATING OF JAPANESE CARS

EXCELLENT
(Standard Shift — Regular Gas Preferred)

Datsun, all models . . . . 1965 on up (*)
Honda Civic (not CVCC) . . . . 1975 on up
Honda Civic CVCC . . . . All Years
Honda Accord . . . . All Years
Toyota, all models . . . . 1967 on up (*)
Subaru, all models . . . . All Years (*)
Dodge Colt . . . . 1973 on up

(*) See exceptions in Average or Poor Categories.

GOOD
(Standard Shift — Regular Gas Preferred)

Datsun 610 . . . . All Years
Datsun F-10 . . . . All Years
Datsun 260 Z . . . . All Years
Dodge Colt 1971-72
Plymouth Arrow . . . . All Years

RATING OF JAPANESE CARS (Continued)

AVERAGE

Honda Civic 1973-1974
Mazda Mizer .... All Years
Mazda GLC .... All Years
Mazda Cosmo .... All Years
Subaru 1100 & 1300 ...... to 1972

POOR

Datsun 1600 Rdstr. Cnvrt. . All Years
Datsun 2000 Rdstr. Cnvrt. . All Years
Honda 600 Sedan .... All Years
Toyota Crown .... All Years
Mazda Rotary RX 2-4 .... All Years
Mazda 618, 808 .... All Years

Sweden

Sweden's two cars, the **Saab** and the **Volvo**, are well-known in the United States. The first Saab came to this country in the form of a front-wheel drive, 3 cylinder two-stroke (gas-oil mix) car. In order to meet the 1968 federal emissions standards, Saab purchased the German Taunus V-4 engine which proved to be a very fine choice. In 1971 the Modell 99 emerged with Triumph power, followed a year later by a fuel injected 99E engine. Saab also builds a fiberglass sports car called the *Sonett*.

Volvo made its first impression in the U.S. market with its Ford-sedan-styled PV 444 in the mid-1950's, followed by an improved 544 made until 1966. Also, in the late 50's the model 120 appeared and sold very well. In 1968 the popular 122 was superceded by the larger and heavier 140 Series. Currently, the expensive 240 and 260 Series are being manufactured.

RATING OF SWEDISH CARS

EXCELLENT
Volvo 122 series . . . . 1962-1968 B-18 eng. std.

GOOD
Saab 95 and 96 . . . . 1967-1970 V-4 engine
Volvo 140 . . . . 1969-1972 B-20 eng std.
Volvo P1800 . . . . up to 1970

AVERAGE
Volvo 140 series 1967-1968
Volvo 140 series . . . . 1971-1974 fuel injected
Volvo 160 series . . . . All Years
Volvo 1800 ES . . . . All Years
Volvo 544 . . . . 1962-1966 B-18 engine
Volvo 240 series . . . . All Years

POOR
Saab, 99 series . . . . All Years
Saab Sonett . . . . All Years
Saab, 3-cylinder . . . . All Years
Volvo . . . All Automatics . . . to 1974
Volvo 122 series . . . . All Years with B-16 engine

Trucks

Now and then I'm asked a question or two about trucks, and my opinion of the various makes. Here's a very brief section on the subject.

Domestic Trucks

The trucks built by the Big Three, GMC, Ford and Chrysler, generally have shown a better service record than those built by International and AMC Jeep, especially among the four-wheel drive vehicles.

Chevy, GMC, Ford and Dodge trucks of the late 60's and early 70's seem best, and a four-speed V-8 is by far the best equipment you could ask for. A long-bed is also desireable and increases the value of the truck.

Foreign Trucks

Imported pick-ups including the Datsun, Toyota, Mazda, Ford Courier and Chevy Luv are all manufactured in Japan. Small trucks from Chrysler are also Japan built.

The Datsun and Toyota long beds are still the best buy in this market. Attention is currently on the newer 4-wheel drive pickups by Chevy, Datsun and Toyota. The Toyota "Jeep", the *Land Cruiser*, is excellent.

Domestic Vans

Vans are the rage these days but no manufacturer has yet produced an exceptionally good one. Most owners record a long list of minor and major nuisances. Given a choice, I'd probably pick a Ford or Dodge van in the three-quarter ton range, with a four-speed transmission. Vans made after 1966 are best.

Foreign Vans

The only foreign van presently available on the used car market is the Volkswagen, and I think it's a terrible vehicle, as it always has been. I strongly recommend all true van lovers to buy American.

Motorcycles and Mopeds

Quite a few people have been looking to the two-wheelers as a practical way to beat the gasoline crisis, so I thought to mention a few things in general.

In the small street bike field, Japan is the obvious leader, and in the larger road bikes, the Japanese bikes and the BMW are by far *the only real choices* for folks who want reliable long distance transportation.

I have a particular dislike for Mopeds, which are both impractical and unsafe. They have neither the speed or the agility of a motorcylce; yet they are even more vulnerable. Driving one only gives the operator all the disadvantages of two-wheel transportation, with only a few more mpg than a 125 cc motorcylce. I hope that people will look at Mopeds for what they really are . . . a nice toy for putting about the yard, but never a machine to duel with other vehicles on our highways. A street bike is far better in all ways. Motor scooters, such as those manufactured by Vespa, are also not recommended.

American Built Cherries Hall Of Fame

Dodge Dart	1963-1969
Plymouth Valiant	1963-1969
Chevrolet Chevy II.	1964-1967
Chevrolet, Full Size	1955-1956
Ford Falcon	1964-1967
Ford Mustang	1964-1966
Ford Fairlane	1965-1967
Checker	1959-1964

YOUR FINANCES

"Banking may be a career from which no man really recovers."

John Kenneth Galbraith

I'd like to talk to you for a while about money. Now, don't get all excited. I don't want to borrow any. I simply want to go over with you some of the possible hidden expenses that you might encounter before you even begin to drive you newly acquired used car.

In these modern times, one does not just buy a car by writing a check and then driving off into the sunset (or in the general direction of where the sunset ought to be, if one lives in a large city). Life, unfortunately, is not so simple anymore. There are a number of things that you have to make allowances for, or you will quickly be in over your head even before you get your hands on the ignition keys.

You recall, I trust, the sad story of Lizzie in Chapter Two? Especially the part where she had to call home for money to pay for registering and licensing the car. Of course you aren't going to make the same mistakes as she did, since you already have much more information at your disposal; however, there's still the matter of working out a financial plan *before* you purchase the car of your choice, and this plan applies no matter what type of car you wish to buy.

Simply put: If you have $1,500 to spend for a used car, don't even think of buying a $1,500 car, because you won't have enough money. For instance, a $1,500 car in superb, wonderful, exquisite condition that *only* needs a set of tires is not actually a $1,500 car. It's more like a $1,600 car, at least. Then after Sales Tax and Registration costs, it's probably a $1,700 automobile. These expenses will be closely followed by the first installment on insurance, which is mandatory in most states, and then perhaps some miscellaneous maintenance fees, like an oil change, wiper blades, maybe a few bulbs. We're now up to nearly $1,800, and the used car hasn't moved more than ten miles yet. All in all, the extra expenses that go along with buying a used car might add up to almost 20% of the car's inital cost.

Is there any way to avoid these extra expenses? Not really. The whole idea of this brief chapter is to remind you of these things, rather than telling you of cheap tricks to beat these hidden costs. You might, however, *minimize* these added expenses by taking some logical steps; be quick thinking, and by all means, do some serious comparative shopping whenever possible.

Sales Tax

Unfortunately, you cannot find any super deals in this category since all states have their own fixed rates of charging Sales Tax. However, you might save *some* money if you get a written Bill Of Sale from the prevous owner to prove the purchase price to the tax people. Very often, if you do not possess a Bill Of Sale, you will be taxed directly by the *book value* of the car you just bought, no matter what price you actually paid for it. Clearly, if you paid more for the vehicle, this works in your favor, but in most cases, the sale price is usually less. It is well recognized that the kind and loving tax officers will, by any means necessary, make you pay the tax based on the book price. At the common rate of 6% or so, the absence of a written Bill Of Sale could cost you a substantial sum of money, so keep this in mind.

Insurance

Next to the tax people, I like the insurance companies the best. A recent report issued by Consumer Action of San Francisco reveals that the premiums charged for the *same exact* insurance coverage and for the same class of drivers varies widely from company to company in the State of California. No doubt, this variation exists throughout the United States, so it is quite possible that the insurance agent you first contact might quote you a price of, say $350 for everything you need, while another agent (who might represent an even more reliable insurance company in terms of claims adjustment) might give you the same package for as little as $220 per year.

It certainly pays to snoop around the insurance scene before obtaining any coverage. It may even be a good idea to line up two or three prospective insurance companies (through their agents) before you buy your used car, so that you will have an accurate measure of just how much to budget for the insurance costs. Some companies, for instance, allow payments in four installments without added interest charges, while others charge you interest or demand the whole payment in one lump. There are also several insurance companies that reward (or penalize) insurance policies depending on the type of car being insured.

Make a few calls before you buy your car. You will never have any problems in getting these friendly agents to talk with you about the kind of coverage you should have. But always keep in mind, the large companies did not accumulate their vast wealth and tremendous skyscrapers by paying claims. It is in *their* interest to sell insurance policies and minimize *their* risks, not yours.

Shopping For Money

To this point, I have avoided mentioning the process of financing a used car for two very good reasons. First, it is very difficult these days to even get financing from a bank or legitimate loan company for most used cars over five years old. This means that unless you are shopping in the 2,000+ range, forget it. The likelihood of getting a loan is not very good unless you are personally very tight with your banker. Second, I have never encouraged people to buy a used car on credit because of the obvious risks involved. Of course, I realize that many people *must* buy a car in this manner, but I still like to urge you to save as much as possible for a large down payment, and then finance only as much as you must. This is not the usual advice given by writers of "How To Make Your Money Grow" books, where the seemingly basic rule is to buy on credit, pay back with inflationary dollars, and invest your savings into some high-yielding something or other, and all that good stuff about money.

Somehow, I just don't feel really good about an economy based on credit and paper profits, and I would, therefore, suggest that if you are out to buy a used car, keep this kind of spending to a bare minimum. Perhaps buying a house on a mortgage is unlike this kind of penny-pinching thought, especially when one considers that a house seems to *increase* in value annually, while a used car is always losing its cash-value. Also, to have a car break down while you're still paying for it is a very dismal situation. I would rather see someone buy a car for cash and then take out loans to restore it to top-notch condition. Then, at least, you will know exactly where your money went, and you might also have some warranties on the restoration repairs to fall back upon.

Returning to the original point of shopping for money, you should always check with more than one bank or loan company on their current interest rates. These rates often differ by a considerable margin, and you might save a hundred dollars or more on a car loan merely by picking the right place to borrow the money.

FIVE

THE SEARCH

I was confused by an ad that read: "Why go elsewhere to get cheated? You can trust us to do the job."

It isn't very likely that you will sit outside your house and wait for the car of your dreams to drive past with a "For Sale" sign on it, yet that's just about as much energy as some people are willing to exert. I hope that you feel more ambitious than that because it has been my experience that the best used cars go to people who spend the most time and effort in hunting them down.

Of course, ambition alone is not enough. You must also know where to find all these wonderful used cars that I've been telling you about, and, you must have a logical method that allows you to cover a good deal of the used car territory, quickly and efficiently. Some places are worth looking into, and some are not. Here are just several suggestions of where to look.

Reading Classified Ads

Some of the best buys in used cars come from private individuals who advertise in either local daily newspapers, weekly free shoppers, university newspapers, or the popular "buy and sell" ad-rags that are passed about free to supermarkets or dumped on people's doorsteps.

Automotive classifieds have a language of their own. These abbreviations are important to learn and remember so that you become familiar with what is being sold. Here is a brief list of the most popular abbreviations that you will encounter. Study them for a minute and maybe they will help you go through listings more rapidly.

as is	the car needs repairs of some kind
auto., (a/t)	automatic transmission
a/c	air conditioning
b.o., best	best offer gets the car (not always money)
e/c, a--1 sharp	excellent condition, car in top-condition
lo. mi.	low mileage
o.d.	overdrive transmission
p/s, p/b	power steering, power brakes
snrf, s/r	sunroof

std., stick	standard transmission
3 spd, 4 spd	standard transmission with 3 or 4 speeds
reblt	rebuilt (one of the most abused words of the English language)

Once you have mastered and translated these ad terms, you will have to evaluate whether the advertised automobile is really worth pursuing or not. This, of course, takes practice, but if you take a look at the samples shown below from some recent automotive ads, you will get some idea of how I operate when I shop around for a good used car.

In selecting through the lists, I have, incidently, already eliminated the "lemons" which were described in Chapter Three. What I'm demonstrating here is how to find the nicest examples of the kind of cars I've already deemed worthwhile.

Group One: Very Good Prospects

NOVA 73 6 cyl auto ps vinyl top exc. cond. gd gas mi beauty car, well-maintained by owner $1700. 555-0592 after 6pm. 555-6566 weekdays. 8-5 pm   11/8/79

74 OPEL Manta like new. $1875 ofr. 555-6327. * * *

68 VW Bug super clean, good engine, low mileage. $1000. 555-8500 * *

OPEL 1900c automatic, exc. clean in and out, low mil. $1500. 555-9137 * *

71 CAPRI, rebuilt engine, new clutch, alternator, paint, new linkage, very clean in and out, must sell because I am moving. * $1100. 555-6544 * *

68 SAAB Wagon reblt tran, new brakes, good and solid $995 or bo. 555-8500 * *

You'll notice that in each of these Group I ads, the owner has taken special care to portray the car as exceptional in some way. Either they are "super clean" or "good and solid" or "like new", etc. Of course, these people may be crazy, but at least you know that you might find a reasonably nice car when you visit them for a closer look. (Actually, the prices shown here are high enough that the cars should, indeed, be something special.)

Group Two: Possible Bargains

DODGE Dart 65; nw rad tires carb, wt. pump, bat, altnatr, volt reg, run smooth; has oil leak? $450. Call Al. 555-7836

69 DATSUN 510 eng., trans. good minor wk $280 eves. Call 555-7921 * * *

64 DODGE Dart 6 cyl std. good car $490 bo. 555-4902

VW Bug 67 v. gd. run cond. blue. $600. 555-9447 bob * *

67 PONTIAC Lemans good condition $350 555-0326 or 555-8201 Anna *

The cars in this group are harder to spot. They are generally low-priced workhorses that may have lost some of their exterior beauty but still possess lots of life and a very modest price tag. No doubt some of the cars shown in this group are not really as good as their owners say, but if cheap transportation is what you want, these are well worth checking out. You'll notice that in each of these ads the owner seems to think that the car is at least worth the look.

Group Three: A Waste of Time

1963 PUEGEOT 404 mechanic's spec. recent valves & clutch, needs new brake, cylinders, you tow. $150. 555-7774 * *

64 BUG runs good, body rough. $400. 555-7239 Bob *

CAPRI 74 4 spd w/ac, snrf, am/fm ster cass. Fair cnd, $2200. Aft 7 pm. 551-8769.

66 VW BUS good engine. Needs work. $500 or best offer. 555-8888 days 555-6790/5-1 pm. Carl

67 MERCEDES auto p/s p/b elec. snrf, radials, nu brake sys. nds some work. $2450/offer. 553-9216 eves/wknds.

The cars of Group Three show very little promise of anything but headaches. The VW's are all very much overpriced (a "rough" body usually means demolished). The Peugot seems to be what I call a "Bail-out," whereby the poor owner, after putting in both engine and transmission work, still can't get the damn thing out of the driveway. The Capri is very expensive for a 1974 car in only "Fair condition". And that Mercedes is strictly for people who have loads of money to pump into repairs and parts.

New Car Dealers

Whenever a new car dealer takes in a customer's used car on trade against a new model, the dealership has to make a quick decision of whether to retain and recondition the trade-in, or wholesale it to a local used car dealer. This decision is made on the basis of the traded car's appearance and mechanical soundness   Contrary to what people think, the vast majority of new car dealers do not sell defective, or cleverly "patched up" vehicles. As a rule, the used cars that they sell are very clean, in very sound condition, and very expensive.

Why do the used cars at an authorized dealership cost so much more than those sold by private individuals? There are many reasons, some obvious, some not.

For one, the new car dealers are very prosperous capitalists who didn't get that way by giving away cars as a charitable gesture. Perhaps a kinder view of their pricing should include mention that they often spend quite a bit of money repairing and "detailing", that is, cleaning, washing, re-upholstering, painting and replacing the chrome.

Another added attraction they provide is some kind of written warranty, either partial (often 50%) or full 100%, on most of the automobiles they sell. Of course, getting satisfaction on some guarantees can be difficult, but at least you do have something on paper, and you do know that most dealers would find it difficult to split town over the weekend. Naturally, someone has to pay for the occasional used car that the dealer takes a loss on in a warranty settlement, and that someone is you.

My general feeling about shopping at a new car dealership for the used car of your dreams is that you ought to consider it, but only after you have exhausted the private party sector through their want ads. And if you elect to buy a car from a new car dealer, expect to pay more for the car you want, but don't throw your money away (see the section "How much should you pay?" at the end of this chapter).

Used Car Dealers

The typical used car dealer is not in any way affiliated with the sale of new cars. He or she is an independent seller of automobiles acquired from a myriad of sources, such as: new car dealers, auctions, rental fleets, private parties, and sometimes even the quick purchases from the guys in leather coats, sunglasses and names like Buddy and Ace. The source of their used products is not nearly as significant as to whom they will be sold.

Many used car dealers keep a hefty supply of worn-out cars on their lots in order to make their selection appear greater than it actually is. These cars are often not road worthy, but in comparison, the cars that are actually for sale often look so much better, that the prospective buyer is immediately impressed by the used cars for sale.

The problem of shopping for a used car through any used car dealer is not that they are all out to cheat you. It would be a very simple but an unfair generalization to accuse these fine merchants of the pre-owned car market of the fraud and deception which is, in fact, practiced only by a few in their business. More often than not, the bad reputation that has been their trademark is caused by the inferior quality of the merchandise and their own genuine lack of knowledge about the cars that they sell. It may come as some surprise that many used car dealers possess no skill whatsoever in understanding the mechanical workings of the modern automobile. They know how to buy them and how to sell them, and in a very rudimentary hit or miss way, they often know how to fix some things (like putting Bardhall in radiators, replacing fuses, and an occasional light bulb), but as a general rule their technical knowledge is frighteningly limited.

It takes some rather sophisticated diagnostic abilities to correctly assess the condition of all systems operating on a car built within the last ten years or so; and if you would agree that many mechanics do not have these abilities, how are salesmen supposed to attain or have them? Therefore, it is not uncommon for a used car dealer to unwittingly pass off a defective automobile to his customer, or, if you want to be less kind, you might say that it isn't unusual for a used car dealer to keep his interest in mechanical things to a minimum. If the engine seems a little rough, and no one is around to further investigate, he just sells the car and keeps his fingers crossed. Sometimes it's only a bad spark plug wire, and sometimes the engine destroys itself in a few months. It's all in the game.

Aside from the unfortunate tendency to believe that too much knowledge is a dangerous thing, used car dealers can also be faulted on the overall quality of their merchandise, which is a reality of their trade. There was a time when a used car dealer could buy a pretty decent car from an authorized dealer or private auction, but those days are fast disappearing. The reason for this is that the "big buck" new dealerships, and a few (very few) big-time used car dealers, are keeping more and more of the kind of cars which smaller dealerships could easily sell to the public. In this manner the new car dealers are investing a greater amount of money into their used merchandise than they have in the past, and are getting higher prices. Meanwhile, the "leftovers" are usually thrown into the arena for smaller used car dealers (at inflated prices) to fight over.

These "leftovers" are not usually very impressive, but once in a while the new car dealer might let go of a nice car, and then, only as a "package" deal. Thus the smaller used car dealer has to take two or three scrap heaps along with the nicer car. These junkers might be seriously damaged or defective in some way, or they might just be "heavy metal", big, unattractive, gas-guzzling cars that have little chance of being quickly sold in today's economy and style-minded car market.

The current famine of good used cars leaves the used car dealer in a double-bind, and quite frankly, it looks like the end of the road for all but the very largest of them. It's increasingly difficult for them to sell complicated, yet second-rate cars without getting into serious trouble, either financially or legally. No wonder some of them behave as badly as they do! It's a case for survival of the fittest, and the fittest aren't always the nicest.

This rather bleak and pessimistic overview of the used car sales industry doesn't exclude the possibility of finding a good car on one of their used car lots (with pinwheels and little lights). Indeed, you are urged to check this scene out, for often the entertainment value itself is well worth the time, and you just might find a bargain. By all means, exercise care and be prepared to walk around many lots. You will bypass a lot of junk, but keep in mind that you might do OK.

Public Auctions

The recent growth and popularity of automobile auctions really puzzle me. Before I started going to them I was like many other bargain-hunting enthusiasts. My mouth watered with envy each time I listened to yet another story of someone picking up a fantastic luxury liner or sports racer for a *ridiculously* low price.

How is it that I have never actually seen such a thing happen? I'm sure that, once in a while, it does; but then again, "once in a while" someone falls out of a ten story building, lands on a passing mattress and sells the rights to TV.

A more likely occurrence is that a few dozen overanxious people get fired up by the frenzy of a very seductive auctioneer. "Folks, I just can't let this car go for that price! Do I hear $500? $500, anybody? Now folks, somebody better call the police, 'cause there's a robbery going on here!", are often the resounding words at these automobile auctions. The prophetic ghost in the machine pours out its warning of a robbery, even before the auction begins. As always, someone starts, and the bidding goes on wildly for a car that was probably stolen, abandoned, repossessed, or used to chase the enemies of the State through the streets of San Francisco.

I may be slightly dogmatic about this, but when all things are considered, I have found that automobile auctions are mostly for gamblers and speculators, amateurs and the heavy-buck professionals, among whom the probability of finding a good used car, for any sane individual, is mighty slim indeed. The odds seem much better in blackjack.

Some Other Hiding Places

Once you have exhausted all of the common sources for the cherry of a used car, it's time to do a little fancy footwork and seek out the less obvious places where a good used car might turn up.

The bulletin boards at local schools, supermarkets, post offices, restaurants and laundromats have always been worth a detailed look, especially for automobiles in the under $1,000 category. I find that ads stuck on a wall somewhere tend to be much more honest and descriptive than ads in the newspaper, yet they often receive far less attention from the general public. Some of the very best cars that I have ever owned came from my patient inspection of wall to wall index cards decorating one side of a college cafeteria. In fact, on a few occasions, I actually put up an ad myself saying that I'd like to buy a certain car at a certain price (and I was always a little cagey about how much).

Another interesting place to look for cars is on the road. Suburban areas are especially ripe for locating used cars for sale; particularly the main highways leading into town, where homeowners have their newer cars already garaged. Their older, used car is left out on the lawn or driveway with a "for sale" sign in the rear window. Some towns have regulations against this practice but many areas across the country are heavily populated with 3rd and 4th cars which are often for sale. It's quite possible to spot a clean and fairly priced car, just sitting out there in the real world with a sign on it, and if it passes you at 55 mph. you know immediately that it can't be all that bad, right? (Follow that car!)

How Much Should You Pay?

I cannot overemphasize the importance of carefully figuring the approximate *market value* of the car being considered before embarking on the search. I realize that this may be difficult, especially if you have a few different models and years in mind; but if you don't get it worked out beforehand, you might end up paying the same price for a 1971 car as you would for a 1974 model, thereby, cheating yourself out of your hard earned cash.

The selling price of cars is often determined by supply and demand. For example, a 1964-1966 Ford Mustang may sell for *more* money than most cars of the same years because it seems that everyone wants one. These desirable cars, are well contrasted by cars like the Chevy Vega and the Mazda Rotary, which sell for far less than the average price mainly because their reputations are not exactly flattering.

Another factor in a car's value is *the condition*, and of course you should keep in mind that an exceptionally nice car can and should sell for more money than the average book value.

You may well ask what all these "books" actually are that get mentioned whenever car prices come up? There is no simple book by which car prices are established. The most popular reference is the "Blue Book" which receives its imaginative name from its non-descript blue paper cover. This little pocket-sized publication is used by most dealers, banks, and insurance companies for the purpose of determining the current (monthly) average selling price of automobiles about six years and newer. In addition to the selling price, the book contains values for the average wholesale and loan prices of all domestic and imported makes. As a rule, the little blue book accurately reflects the prices realized in the day to day business of buying and selling cars throughout the country.

Whenever anyone talks about the "book" price of a car, please keep in mind that the average selling (retail) price shown is for automobiles in top-notch condition, almost perfect, with normal mileage and equipment. If you see an automobile in lesser condition, don't let someone's finger pointing to a blue book retail price bother you a bit — they are asking far too much! Ideally, a good buy on a used car would be somewhere between the wholesale and and retail prices given. The *loan value* entry is also useful information, in case you ever plan to finance the car which you want to buy. It will tell you how much the bank will probably loan you on it (again in top-notch condition).

Since the "Blue Book" is a bit hard to obtain, sold only by subscription to people who read them like a poker hand, you might consider buying a copy of *Edmund's Used Car Prices*, available at most local newstands or by writing to Edmund's Subscription Dept., USC-478, 515 Hempstead Tpk. West Hempstead, NY 11552. Ask for the current issue and send them $1.95 plus 50 cents ransom money for the U.S.P.S. This book is not used as often as the blue book in professional circles, but it can be useful protection against over-payment for your prospective car.

There are some automobiles that are not listed in the pricing books. These include: (1) Cars that are over seven years old, and (2) Cars so wierd that they exclude normal mainstream interests (e.g. 1975 Bradley). In the case that your car is not listed in these books, the best approach is to read the Classified Ads in as many newspapers as possible and through careful sampling, arrive at an expected selling price. For instance, if you want to buy a 1971 Datsun 510, and you have found two 1972's selling for $1,200 and $1,300 respectively, and a 1970 for $774; you should (correctly) guess that your price is near to $1,000 for a nice, clean 1971 model. This kind of estimating does not work the same way for all cars. If your choice were a Volvo, it would be higher (don't ask me why), whereas if your choice were a Ford Pinto, it would be less (far less) and rightly so. Again the rules of "supply and demand" dictate, as well as the car's overall condition. So, an exceptionally clean 1971 Datsun 510 (with very low mileage) might demand as much as $1,500, while the worn rusted version of the same year may only be valued at $300.

As a general rule, you should pay as much for your used car as everyone else seems to be paying, according to all the information you can gather from the blue book and newspapers. Don't let the speculator, the greedy dreamer, or the automobile myth-maker deceive you. If there were anything you can surely say about a used car, any used car, it is probably that there is a similar car for less money just around the corner.

The Telephone Makes It Easier

A basic problem in shopping for a used car is that it can become very tiring. It is so very easy to burn-out, get tired, and then begin to compromise your original thoughts about what used car to finally buy. This psychological fatigue can become very wearing on the best of us; especially after several days of circling Classified Ads, dialing strange phone numbers, following complicated directions to streets that even cabbies rarely hear about, lifting countless hoods, listening to everyone's sales pitch, sad stories, politely escaping from disappointing encounters ("come back tomorrow and I'll have the brakes fixed and the radiator soldered . . ."), and anxiously waiting for the "right" deal to be made. Under such strain, it is tempting to simply buy a car, any car, quickly to end all the hassle. This aspect of irreducible haste is perhaps the greatest factor in common to all used car buyers. Remember, the time that you "save" while shopping for a good used car will be collected over and over again in break-downs, roadside repairs, and long waits at strange service stations. You must keep in mind that to compromise is a lofty principle, but to act passionately or with empathy for the car's seller, is foolish. Unless you intend to buy a used car every month or so, take your time.

 There are several ways to make the search for a used car less painful, the most important of which is to use the telephone to its fullest. You have already learned how to be selective in reading the Classified Ads, and thus to eliminate the least promising cars. Now you can ensure that your time will not be wasted by simply asking the *right questions* when placing a phone inquiry about a used car.

 The process of communicating over the phone is, again, not overly involved. Let's face it. It is not computer - dating, and most likely, unless you are a very lonely soul, you're not going to develop a lifetime friendship with the person you are trying to buy a used car from. So, why pitter-patter about on the psychological/social eggshell of formalities? Get efficient and business-minded in making the contact. *You* have the bucks, the other person has the car, and in a very real way, you have the advantage over the seller. So why not get tough? Not impolite certainly, but rather *to the point*. For example:

    Question 1: How long have you owned the car?
    Question 2: Why are you selling it?
    Question 3: Is it very rusty?
    Question 4: Does it burn oil?
    Question 5: Does it need repairs? What kind?
    Question 6: Does it need extensive bodywork?

Note all the information and decide quickly if it is worth your time to pursue this car any further. Don't plan on seeing more than two good prospects in any given day, and remember, don't let impatience get the best of you.

SIX

CHECKING IT OUT

To find the actual running time of a car, divide the miles shown on the odometer by 1,000 to get the age in days driven. So, a car with 30,000 miles has only one month of real time on the highway.

A careful examination of the used car you expect to buy is the single, most relevant thing you will do. If you slack-off at this point, and get careless or impatient, it will matter little whether you know which cars are the "cherries" and which ones are the "lemons" (bitter fruit). No car in poor condition is a "cherry" in anyone's book, even if once, long ago, the model was hailed as an automotive gem. This book's value is informing you how to avoid getting burned, but unless you take it seriously, and take the necessary steps to make sure *your* used car is, indeed, in good mechanical shape, all of your preliminary scanning, planning, and work will be wasted.

Before considering the steps for inspecting your future car, it is essential that you are able to answer the following three important questions:

1. Do you know the car (or cars) that you would most like to buy? Make, model, year?
2. Do you know *exactly* how much money in dollars and cents, (including all the hidden expenses mentioned earlier,) you can afford to spend?

3. Do you know the approximate market value of the car (or cars) that you might want to buy?

You should be able to lay all this information out in front of you, perhaps like this:

1. I want a clean Datsun 510 Station Wagon (1970-1972).
2. I can afford up to $1,525.00 for the purchase.
3. According to the prices I've seen, this car should cost from $700 to $1400.

If you cannot answer these three questions at this time, then there is little reason for you to proceed in checking out *any* used car. For no matter how good the deal sounds, you are not getting what you want. Even if you buy a used car simply because it "sounds like a good deal" and miraculously avoid getting fried, you will still not be happy because it will not be *the* car that you may want. Clearly, the beginning point is for you to choose and select your goal carefully, and if you can't answer these three vital questions, simply go back and gather the necessary information until you can. I cannot overstate the importance of this issue, for it is the keystone to successfully buying any used car.

If you *can* answer these three important questions, I would suggest that you sleep on it for at least one night. Too often, we all make some mistake, and unless you are quite certain of your actual wants, it makes good sense to not hurry. So, review your alternatives remembering that there are several different kinds of good used cars. Even if you think this is a childish or boring exercise, take your time in fine-tuning your answers to these three questions.

Only after you establish your exact boundaries for the used car you wish to purchase, can you proceed to actually examine the real car in a real world.

Examining A Used Car

A proper examination of a used car is done in two steps:
1. You will examine the car you want to buy.
2. A competent mechanic will examine the car, only after the car receives high marks from you.

Checking out a used car twice in this manner will generate enough information for you to be fairly confident in your purchase. I am assuming that you and I can lay the groundwork for finding a good used car for you, but that guarantees you very little. *I have the bucks for the book*, and you may now have learned something about buying a good used car. Practical limits restrain us from making you a crack-mechanic, and any detailed information about cars would probably turn you away from reading this book anyway. So, an outside consultant seems necessary. Someone who knows all those subtle things; noises, test results, visual observations, etc., that only a qualified mechanic can really tune-in on.

Most magazine articles, or consumer pamphlets, that boast to "help" people examine a used car are quite useless. At best, these "consumer tips" ask you to look silly and do a bunch of dubious things that make mechanics chuckle. Here's one small example:

> Check to see if the brake pedal is excessively worn. If it shows more wear than is likely for a car with low mileage, chances are the speedometer on the car has been altered.

This is nonsense. It's difficult enough for most people to even find the speedometer cable on newer automobiles (it is for me), much less have the expertise to recalibrate (turn back) an odometer. Besides, who cares what mileage a car has? If a car runs well and is solid, chances are that it will give you long and faithful service.

You will have to perform the first important inspection of the used car. Even if you know very little about automobiles, this exam will enable you to save the time and expense of dragging a mechanic to every used car that you think of buying. While you should have enough information to make this initial inspection, remember that you alone cannot make the final evaluation of a used car's mechanical worthiness. This is not to say that you cannot make an evaluation and act upon it, but rather, the applied value of your judgment is over-extended unless you, yourself are a mechanic.

The automotive industry encourages weekend mechanics to do things like change spark plugs, change the oil and filter, add antifreeze, and repair tears on vinyl seat upholstery. It is fast becoming an American tradition to be "handy" around cars, but you will notice that in most of these cases, the manufacturer of some gadget or replacement part wants simply to sell you things. What happens to those items is secondary to your purchase of them (be it spark plugs, oil at $.68/qt, or super glue); it is almost all "techno-hype" which encourages folks to brave some minor repairs. However, when it comes to the heavy-duty work of automobile maintenance and repair, few would propose an alternative to having the work done by a competent automobile mechanic.

In the same way, we must separate incidentals from the core of the issue. You want to buy a good used car. *You*, therefore, must treat any prospective used car as an investment and gain adequate consultation from someone whose livelihood is tied to automotive repair, even if, the seller is a little old school teacher about to go on Social

Security pension. Remember, the final o.k. should be entrusted to a reliable mechanic.

If I were shopping in an area about which I knew very little, for instance sailboats, I would be sure to consult an expert before I made my purchase. But I wouldn't ask him to look at a boat that was sinking. So, don't get overly paranoid in trusting your own abilities.

You should aim to feel confident, somewhere between incompetent and overconfident, with a keen eye and your senses in tune. The following **CHECKLIST I,** offers some gentle guidelines; you should learn about the most important variables involved and then proceed to check-out the used car.

Checklist I
(For The Buyer)

Part A: Eyeballing The Car

This part should be done in peace, quiet, and relative tranquility, without the seller or dealer yapping in your face. Imagine yourself as a Zen Master, searching for inner zeros, and request a period of absolute silence from anyone around you. Preferably to be left alone with the car. When you are relaxed and peaceful, look at the car. Think about the traffic jams it will get you through. Imagine driving it about your normal daily tour, not the one-time yearly vacation to Peoria. Let the car speak for itself to you. Walk around it slowly with the prime idea of noticing things that are obviously wrong, things that might cost you money to repair (either immediately, or in terms of resale value).

☐ *Look at the tires.* Are the treads well grooved? New or even used tires will cost a good deal of money. Remember, the larger the tires, the more expensive they are, and often harder to find on the market (14 inch tires are most popular).

☐ *Look for broken or chipped glass,* or cracked turn-signal and brake light lenses. Very often you'll have to replace them immediately as they are illegal and could cost you a ticket plus replacement.

☐ *Look for a valid State Inspection sticker.* If the car does not have one, you will have to pay for one, and maybe meet a tough inspector who will gain great joy in forcing you to restore the car to "factory specs" rather than just a normal "passable" condition. If the sticker is due within a short period from the date, you may consider the car as though it is not inspected and think about why the seller is now unloading the car.

☐ *Look at the body.* Are there many rusty seams or places that have been rusted through? Some states require that *all* rust holes be absent (like Pennsylvania, which also conducts inspections twice yearly). Developing rust means that the car will never be worth very much and will surely deteriorate through time. Rusty cars attract the attention of every State Patrol of every state in the immediate universe, so don't ignore rust as a variable in deciding to buy the used car.

☐ *Look for body damage.* Are there any nasty crush-type dents that require replacement? Body work is neither easy nor cheap, and affects the overall appearance of the car. All cars sell by their attractiveness, no matter how well they run. Look at the way the car sits. Is it level? Does it lean excessively to either side, or forward? Make a note of this.

☐ *Now only after a time of just looking, open the driver's door.* Sit inside. Does the car feel, look (and smell) as if it has had much care? Do the seats look like they have recently been machine gunned? Stomp your foot once. Is the floor board solid?

☐ *Start the engine.* Does the Oil Light and/or Oil Gauge work? If not, *STOP RIGHT THERE!* Tell the owner to fix it or forget it. (You cannot afford to take a chance on something that crucial!) If the Oil Light responds quickly (within 15 seconds), let the engine run for several minutes. (During this time you can check the windshield wiper or the radio.) With the engine still running, get out and open the hood.

☐ *Listen to the motor.* Is it seemingly loud? I mean, really loud and clattery? Is the motor greasy? (You can always tell if an engine has been recently steam-cleaned; look at the bottom of the engine, where all the dirt winds up.) Look under the engine while it is still running. Is there any leaking oil or water?

☐ *Shut the engine off.* Wait a minute and then check the oil. Is it clean and full? If it is low or empty, where did the oil go?

Briefly stop and write down your thoughts about all the things that you saw. You don't have to be very technical (being poetic is also fun). Write down your first impressions of the car, and note your observations of the things that you already know will have to be done (if any).

NOTES:

After this first encounter with a used car, it should be pretty clear whether the car is sending you very strong negative or positive feelings. If you are getting many troublesome impressions, like seeing worn or broken items, smelling oil and gasoline, and hearing odd things around the engine then *THIS IS YOUR INTUITION AT WORK.* Trust yourself! If something looks, feels, smells, sounds terrible, it probably is. If it were something very simple, an honest and conscientious owner would have repaired it, don't you think?

On the other hand, if nothing overly evil seems to be jumping out at you from the car, and if you have noticed no bothersome deficiencies, things may be just swell. Or, you may still have a lemon, but you can't tell yet. At this point, give the car the benefit of your doubts (even if they don't exist) and continue with the inspection. After all, you may in fact have found something very good. Keep in mind, one bad tire and a little dent, or a broken brake lens isn't all that bad for now, so keep on with the inspection if all you found was some $50 worth of minor repairs.

Part B: Cruising (A Test Drive)

This test is all common sense. Again, let your ears, hands and feet open up, and in mental peacefulness, tune-in to the car. Tell the seller to again please remain quiet. They may think you a bit strange for insisting on this, but remember, it's your money and you'll find most people anxious to cooperate.

☐ *Keep the windows open and the radio OFF.* (You can catch the news and tunes later.)

☐ *Start the engine again,* and again notice how the gauges react. Be sure to check these often during the test drive. (A warmer engine always has a lower oil pressure than a cold one, but the pressure should be at least 30 lbs/in at highway speeds.)

☐ *Place the car into gear and take-off briskly.* Do you hear any shuddering vibrations? Knocking at your feet or at the seat of your pants? Are there any horrible noises, clunks, ker-chunks? Does the stick shift move smoothly without sticking, grinding, jamming or popping-out of gear?

☐ *Try the brakes.* Gently depress the pedal and notice any pulling to one side, screeching or heavy scraping sounds. (Ignore tiny squeaks, especially on a car with disc brakes.)

☐ *Does the car steer well?* Will it go straight if you let go of the wheel? (Careful!). Find a stretch of road with bumps or railroad tracks to cross. (Careful!). Does the steering wheel shake excessively, almost jumping out of your hands? Does the car "bottom-out" as if it had bricks rather than shock absorbers underneath? Drive up to highway speed (55 mph). Does the car accelerate smoothly with no bucking or jerking? How does the steering wheel feel at the higher speeds?

☐ *For the final test, find a hill or lots of open, level ground.* Accelerate to a safe 55 mph *and then, just take your foot off the gas pedal.* When you cruise down to 30 mph, punch the gas and either look through the rear view mirror, or have a friend stick his/her head out of the window. You are looking for a cloud of blue smoke exhaust from the tailpipe. Such a cloud originates from the burning of oil, and if you can see it, you are in for big troubles if you buy that car! Even if you see no blue smoke, the mechanic should check this again later. If you don't have enough highway space to try this test safely, an alternative method is to stop the car and stand outside the door with one foot stretched inside to reach the gas pedal. Race the engine while looking back at the tailpipe to spot the blue smoke. Not white, or black, but distinctively blue.

☐ *After the cruise, park the car,* but leave the engine running and open the hood once again. Are there any leaks, up top or underneath? Have new noises developed? Is the temperature noticeably higher? Check the heat gauge for excessive temperature.

☐ *Turn off the engine and once again put into writing your impressions,* just as you did with the Visual Inspection. Take your time to evaluate the important factors that you felt and can remember. WRITE IT DOWN!

NOTES:

_____

_____

_____

_____

_____

_____

_____

_____

_____

_____

    Once again, you must trust your own intuition. Did you enjoy driving the car? Think about the long hours you will spend in it. Perhaps the car was just "o.k.", rather than "fantastic", or a kind that you would like to drive. How did it perform? Was the owner making excuses for things that were obviously wrong? Do you think that the car was cared for?

    At this point, you should be able to reach some conclusions whether to continue in thoughts of buying the car. If all of your impressions were favorable, it is time to call in a mechanic to check the car over for you. Act surely, but not in haste. Keep in mind, that without a deposit, a really good used car will not be around very long. Try to have your mechanic come to see the car on the very same day, again only if you really like the car. If on the other hand, you are still undecided, sleep on it until tomorrow and chance that perhaps someone will buy it before you. Don't Rush!

The Final Examination

If you do not know a reliable mechanic, and no one can recommend one to you, then you may have to rely on passing the prospective car through a local Diagnostic Center. These electronic computers are commonly available for analysis at local garages (especially one that has been in the car-repair business for some time). Although these machines lack the human dimension of analysis, and their operators pass vehicles through as a daily course of events, the modern Diagnostic Center is still the best alternative for anyone needing mechanical information about a prospective used car.

You should be prepared to pay a good mechanic anywhere from $15 to $25 an hour to accompany you and inspect the car. A fair Diagnostic Clinic will charge at least $25 to pass the car through their system. In either case, make sure to get all prices worked out before you agree to hire anyone to do anything.

In Chapter 9, some useful information is given about mechanics in general, but for now, you really don't need a mechanic with whom you expect to develop a long-time working relationship. That will come later, after you buy a car and have had time to settle in with it. You simply need someone who knows enough about cars to spot serious defects that might lead to costly repairs.

A warning about finding a competent mechanic is in order here. Do everything in your power to hire a professional, one who does automotive work as a living, and by all means avoid relying on friends who may at best be "leisure-time" mechanics, or greatly overspecialized with only their kind of car. For example, I know a person who has owned only Volvos for over 18 years, and probably knows every bolt on *only* the models he has owned. He is an excellent mechanic for *his* cars, but when faced with, say, a 1972 Toyota, he would admit being uncertain about how it works. So, keep your friends at a respectful distance, since it is very easy to get fooled. The modern car is a very complex machine and examining one can no longer be entrusted to the tire-kicking old man, kid brother, or amiable "mechanic" friend.

Once you have found a competent person to help you in the Final Inspection, please have them stick their noses here.

A Word With Your Mechanic

Hi! I know that every mechanic has their own way of doing things in checking out a car. My own method is to check the most important things real well, and waste no time on minor items like the lights, wipers, horn, etc. Some of the important things are listed below and I'd like you to use your expert eyes, ears and hands to get a feel for this car. Thanks much for your help.

Checklist II
(For the Mechanic)

Please answer each category Yes or No:

YES NO 1. **ENGINE**
- Start and run well?
- Any blow by?
- Loud tappets?
- Water pump/alternator noises?
- Rod or bearing knocks?
- Front cover or rear main leaks?
- Overheating?

YES NO 2. **TRANSMISSION**
- Clutch or automatic slippage?
- Chattering?
- Throw-out noise/front pump noise?
- Bad leaks?

YES NO 3. **DRIVELINE**
- U-joints o.k.?
- Differential leaks?

YES NO 4. **TEST DRIVE**
- Does the car shift well?
- See any oil burning?
- Any loud drivetrain noises?
- Do brakes feel o.k.?
- Front end seem o.k.?
- Do gauges give good readings?
- Windshield glass o.k.?

YES NO 5. **YOUR OPINION**
__ __   Does this car need a Compression Test?
__ __   A front end visual test?
__ __   A front wheel pulled?
            (If so, will you do these, or tell the buyer
__ __   where to have it done).
            What do you think of this car?

       6. **COMMENTS**

After you and the mechanic have had a little chat you should have your mind well made up about this car. If the Answer is *YES*, your task of buying a good used car seems to be complete, and you should go on to the next chapter of *Cherries and Lemons*.

If it is *"NO!"*, do not regret the decision, but think about all that money you've saved by not getting burned with a bum car. Consider the money spent for the mechanic to be a great bargain!

THE ACTUAL PURCHASE

From 1967 to 1973 the standard new car warranty decreased from two years and 24,000 miles to one year and 12,000 miles.

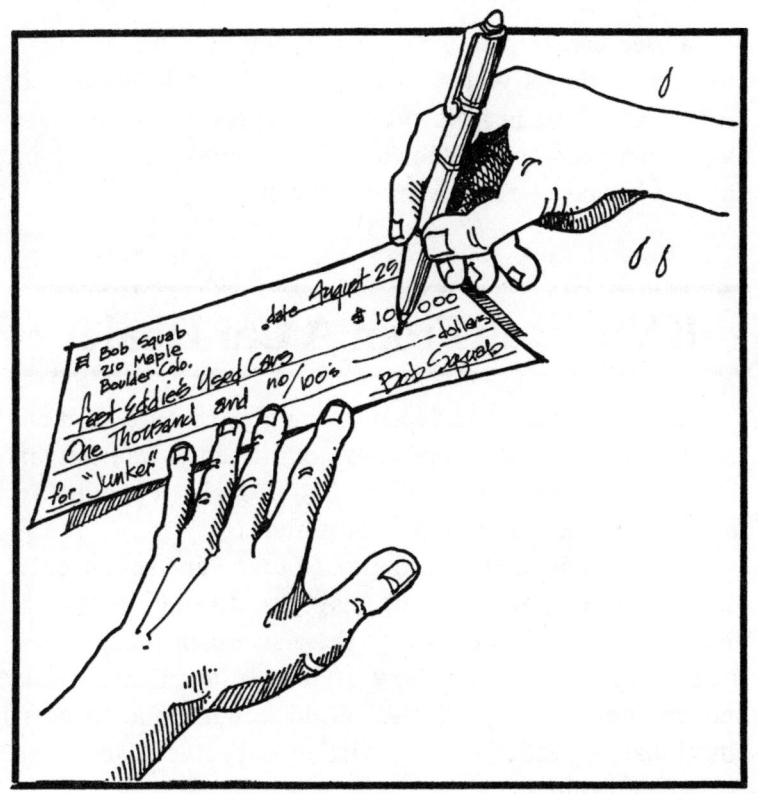

Some of the most costly and unfortunate mistakes that used car buyers make have little to do with the automobile's condition or reputation. These mistakes occur during the actual purchase; either in the negotiations or the subsequent paperwork.

As I mentioned earlier, you don't just toss someone your money in a crumpled ball and then jump behind the wheel and drive away into the sunset. This kind of romantic, carefree attitude, while charming in small doses, or in Clint Eastwood movies, is a thoroughly senseless way to buy a used car. Depending on where you buy the car, there are certain things you must deal with. Keep in mind that I don't claim to be a lawyer, or to speak for your State Department of Motor Vehicles, (I'd be lousy at both jobs anyway because I don't wear neckties.)

If You Buy From A Car Dealer

In most cases, the dealer's asking price on a used car is negotiable, and bargaining is considered a tradition in the used car lots of the United States. Make it a point to squeeze out the best deal you possibly can!

A dealer is in the business of buying and selling cars. Many hundreds of used cars may pass through a typical dealer's lot, which means that these salesmen really know their business. From the flow of deals, adjustments, offers and counter-offers, most dealers do not respond to most emotional appeals, or long winded sob stories, as some private party might.

Don't be silly, giving all sorts of heart-clutching tales of misfortune; cries of shock, anguish and outrage. None will move the dealer to lower the price. You might as well give a Shakespearian soliloque (Hamlet is quite well known) and perhaps gain entrance to a dealer's sense of humor. However, good working knowledge of market values, might move even the most stonewall dealer to think about a lowered price.

What I often do when I'm trying to negotiate a deal with a salesman is to present my opinion of the fair market value for the car. This price is between the retail and wholesale cost as listed in the Blue Book, or, the average price from a dozen newspaper ads for the sale of the same type of car. In addition, I let the dealer know the results of my mechanic's report for all the necessary repairs. The goal in all this is to have the dealer deduct the cost of repairs from a fair market price. It is important to keep in mind, that none of these repairs ought to interfere with any guarantee after the deal is made. All too often a dealer will drop his price and then claim that the lower price was agreed to *in lieu* of a warranty. Be careful!

If the dealer remains obstinate and insists upon selling the used car at what appears to be a high price, you must be prepared to walk away and perhaps check back with the dealer several days later. The salesperson may have "a change of heart" and lower the price, especially if he realizes that you are a serious buyer, rather than a comparative shopper. Remember, *don't ever bargain for a car unless you really want it!* Telling the dealer something like: "I'll give you $1,500 for it this afternoon at 4," may seem very tempting. This is a much more decisive strategy toward bargaining than the casual approach of: "If I were to *possibly* buy this car, would you think about a reduction in the price?" Never use the word "possibly" since we all know that everything is!

Once a price is agreed upon, or if you wish, while you are bargaining for the good price; consider what kind of guarantee comes along with the car. Generally, there are three types of guarantees:

(1) The Full, or, 100% Warranty,
(2) The Fifty-Fifty Guarantee, and,
(3) The Parts-Labor Split Guarantee.

There also is a fourth, infamous "As Is" guarantee which is readily recognized by it's Zero, or absence of, any guarantee. All of these guarantees have in common is their respective liability to the seller for the used car being sold.

The Full (100%) Guarantee

This agreement should say clearly *in writing* that the dealer will repair, with no charge to you the purchaser, any defects in the car within a period of time (maybe 30 days, hopefully 90 days). Some dealers offer a sliding guarantee, in which the first, say, 30 days fall under this kind of Full Guarantee agreement, and later extend into some modified guarantee plan.

The Primary Law of Used Car Buying states that if it is not in writing, it does not exist; it means nothing; nobody ever said it; you misunderstood it; and now that you own it, can we help you push it? (Towing Fee: $25).

Some Full Guarantees *exclude* certain items altogether, or may speak about repairs only to the "Power Train", which in most applications means the engine, transmission, clutch, driveshaft, differential and axles. Therefore, a power train guarantee does not include things like brakes, lights, front end, cooling systems and the like. You should know exactly what is included in your guarantee, and you should insist that it be clearly spelled out in writing. A salesperson's promise to "fix it the next time you drop by . . ." is not a very good guarantee at all. If you buy a car with a broken window, you have in fact, bought a car with a broken window unless its repair is promised in writing in the guarantee contract.

The Fifty-Fifty (50%-50%) Guarantee

This kind of agreement states that in the event of a repair being necessary, you, the owner, agree to pay one-half (50%) of the Total Cost of those repairs, and the dealer agrees to pay the other half of this repair bill. Usually this kind of arrangement can work out quite fairly, however some dealers insist that the repair work *must* be done at the dealer's service station. You should beware (even without my warning), that it would be quite easy for a dealer to raise the normal repair costs, and then charge you half. I'm not suggesting that dealers even consider such a practice; but then, an outstanding dealer would offer a Full 100% Guarantee, don't you agree?

Most 50-50 Guarantees will save you little or nothing, and should not be considered as a significant benefit in your favor. Perhaps this kind of warranty works best when the dealer offers it as an "extended guarantee", whereby an additional 45-60 days of repair service is added to the first 30-90 day Full Guarantee, which is not restricted to the dealer's service station.

The Parts-Labor Split Guarantee

This is merely an agreement where the dealer agrees to pay for *either* the parts or labor required to repair the used car you buy, for again, a limited time (30-90 days). Who pays what isn't often very clear, and in fact, this type of guarantee isn't much better than the 50-50 Guarantee, with all of it's shortcomings. It should be considered as a gimmick to make a deal sound good to you, when it's really of very limited value.

The "As-Is" Guarantee

This is the same as no guarantee. It is equivalent to you admitting to the world that you're buying scrap iron without any expectations that it will run, even for several hours. "AS IS" is a very shaky term legally, and the courts are becoming increasingly sympathetic to the used car buyers who drive an "AS IS" vehicle for one day and then have it blow up on them. The legal reasoning is that anything sold as "junk" should cost very little, and by charging a high price for "AS IS" cars, dealers are implying serviceability. However, you can't always count on such a sympathetic judgment, and therefore you should beware that if you sign an "AS IS" sales contract, you are taking a big risk.

If you are paying a premium price for a used car at a dealership, you should never settle for an "AS IS" declaration on your sales contract. You might as well buy the car from a private party and let dealers like that remain hungry.

Along with a written guarantee, you should always get a Bill of Sale. At the time of purchase, it is a good idea to check the car's Serial Number, making certain that it appears exactly the same on the car and on the Bill of Sale. A reputable dealer supposedly has already done this, but by all means take the time to do it yourself again. Even if the dealer is perfectly straight with you, the numbers might be incorrect anyway, and if there is a discrepancy between the numbers on the car and on the paper, it can be an enormous hassle. Don't take the chance!

Finally, the dealer should arrange some kind of Temporary Registration until your ownership and registration paperwork is complete. In some states, the dealer does all of this for you, while in other states the paperwork is *your responsibility*. If you are in doubt about the proper way to handle automotive paperwork, call your local branch of the Department of Motor Vehicles (listed in the phone book under your State Government). Remember, if the paperwork is not done correctly, there is a possibility that you do not have legal title to the car, and in some cases, you may never get it.

If You Buy From A Private Party

Private individuals rarely offer a guarantee, so your main concern in a purchase of this type is to first of all bargain (of course), and then pay close attention to the paperwork.

Once a fair price is agreed upon, check the Serial Numbers on the car *before* you give anyone money. Do the numbers on the car match the numbers on the owner's registration? If not, *do not* buy the car until the owner can straighten this out with the Department of Motor Vehicles. It may all be a very honest mistake, or it may be a stolen car and can be legally impounded at any time.

After you check the Serial Numbers, ask to see a valid Title to the car *before* you give out any money. In some states, the owner actually has the Title in possession, while in other states, they may only have a copy of the original Title or merely some kind of slip representing ownership. Find out what you must get from the last owner if you are not sure how the system works in your state, or if you're buying an out-of-state used car. Don't *ever* pay for a car without the proper papers, even if the owner swears to bring by that very afternoon (I guess it's ok with someone you know).

Finally, if the Serial Numbers check and the proper papers are shown to you, pay your money and get a written Bill of Sale. You will need this when you go to register the car, since you will, no doubt, have to pay a Sales Tax on the used car. If you have no Bill of Sale, and you bought the car for less than the book value, the tax people will charge you the book value anyway, and *that* could cost you quite a bit of money.

Summary

1. Bargain for a fair price.
2. Know the exact provisions of your Guarantee and get it in writing.
3. Check the car's Serial Numbers against the vehicle's papers.
4. Get the proper Ownership Papers for the car.
5. Get a signed Bill of Sale.
6. Drive your new used car home and read the next exciting chapter of this book!

CARE AND FEEDING

If you drive a brand new American mid-size car, it will cost you approximately 20 cents per mile, or roughly $2,700 per year to operate it. This figure includes gas, oil, maintenance, tires, insurance, license, registration, depreciation and finance costs.

Now that you own a cherry of a used car, you have a responsibility to maintain it. I use this word because there really is an obligation to yourself and others to keep your car running safely and efficiently.

In the following chapter I'll tell you how to save money on parts and repairs, and how to find yourself a good mechanic. But before getting into these things, it seems a good idea to look at car maintenance in general, so that you can guide yourself and your mechanic with an intelligent plan of action for keeping your car in tip-top shape.

If you consider a car as a long-term investment, rather than something to be thrown-off in a few years, then the expense of frequent maintenance is more than worth it. For instance, if you change the oil and oil filter every

2,000 miles as I recommend, it may cost you $250 over a distance of 50,000 miles. Whereas, if you decide to "save" money and change the oil every 5,000 miles, you will save $150 in those 50,000 miles, but you might end up buying an $800 rebuilt engine as a result of such abuse.

Hey, wait a minute! Don't most manufacturers *recommend* oil changes at 3,000, 4,000, or even 6,000 mile intervals? If the factory Service Manuals give that advice, how can it be called "abuse"? Good question. I suppose that it comes down to whether you *believe* the factory is giving you the best advice, or simply telling you the minimally acceptable level at which your car will operate. All I can tell you is what I see when I look at engine oil that's been in there for 5,000 miles. It looks terrible. It is terrible. It should have been changed when it first got filthy, not 3,000 miles after that. Is it worth a few dollars to do that to an engine?

Further evidence of careless maintenance can be found by a quick look at the records of any tow truck service. Most "emergency calls" that are made to assist roadside breakdowns are due to *minor* components failing, like fan belts, leaking hoses, or burned ignition points. In fact, it looks to me like at least 80% of all breakdowns on the road are easily preventable by following a simple maintenance schedule.

As for the number of accidents caused by poor maintenance, that's very difficult to evaluate, since once a car is smashed-up, evidence of mechanical failure is often completely destroyed. From my experience as a mechanic I would say that there are many, many cars on the road today that have substandard brakes and steering systems. In fact, some of the cars are so bad that in an emergency braking or evasion situation, they would probably fail to perform safely.

There is little doubt that good maintenance pays off, and with a little extra effort and imagination, it doesn't have to become a financial burden.

A Good And Simple Maintenance Schedule

The most expensive aspect of this Maintenance Schedule will be during the first months after you purchase your used car. This is probably a good time to spend the money, because you've already been writing lots of checks, and you know that you're investing in the reliability and safety of your new acquisition. There's nothing like starting off on the right foot!

Within the First 60 Days Of Purchasing Your Car

1. Change the oil and oil filter. Check all fluids. Get the car lubricated.
2. Change the transmission and differential fluids if excessively dirty.
3. Check all the belts and hoses in the engine compartment. Replace all that are cracked or defective in any way.
4. Get a good tune-up if necessary and a new air filter.
5. Check the front and rear brakes and have the front wheel bearings re-packed.
6. If it wasn't done before you bought the car, have the front end and exhaust system checked for defects.

I realize that this is a lot of work to have done right away, perhaps close to $200 worth if everything is necessary, but more likely closer to $100-$125. Of course, this work can be spaced out over a period of a few months, and if you avoided an accident or a towing fee because of all the good things you had done for your car, the maintenance bill is very reasonable, don't you think?

Every Week

1. Open the Hood and check your water, oil, battery acid level, and if equipped with an automatic, the transmission fluid (usually checked with the engine hot and running). Poke about under there, look for leaks, corroded battery cables, loose wires and unusual sounds.
2. Check your brake and power steering fluids.
3. With an accurate tire guage, check all five tires for correct air pressure, 25-29 lbs. Check with owner's manual, dealership, or local tire dealer for the proper inflation pressures.

Every 2,000 Miles

1. Change the oil and oil filter. Never leave an old filter on the car when you change your oil. I would recommend something like Castrol GTX 20W-50 in summer, and 10W-50 in cold climates. This is very good oil, although I suppose any brand name will do. When possible, use "Pennsylvania" grade motor oil, as these oils have a longer duration to engine temperatures, and will breakdown to paraffin residues, rather than acid

residues from the non-Pennsylvanian motor oils. Generally, I don't recommend synthetic oils like Mobile One for high mileage engines as yours is likely to be, because synthetic oils are much too expensive for cars old enough to burn or leak oil. If your engine is really tight, and you find a heavy-duty, long distance oil filter to use, then a brand-name synthetic oil such as Mobil One Onc could be of some benefit to you. The synthetic oils are much more slippery than regular oils, they do not easily break down under excessive heat conditions, and they can be used for 15,000 miles without a change, provided that a "depth" filter and not a regular oil filter is used. Be prepared to spend about $4.00 a quart for this kind of oil.

Every 3,000 Miles

Special Note to Volkswagen Bug Owners: Adjust your valves and check the fan belt tension. Do this faithfully or suffer the consequences!

Every 5,000 Miles

1. Check the air filter, and replace it if you cannot easily see light through it.
2. Check and clean the PCV Valve if you have one.
3. All 4-cylinder engineers should have a minor tune-up. These little engines have to work harder than the bigger V-8's and they need a pick-me-up right about now.

Every 10,000 Miles

Return to the first part of this schedule entitled "Within the First 60 Days..." and do all the actions in that list all over again, except, merely check, rather than change the transmission and differential fluids. Special Note to SAAB Owners: Change the transmission fluid now, and every 10,000 miles. On all other cars, drain and flush the cooling system at this time, and service your emission control system.

Every 30,000 Miles

In addition to the usual 10,000 mile service done at this time, change the transmission and differential fluids, and pay someone (or spend the time yourself with wrenches and screwdrivers) to tighten up *everything* on the car that appears to be loose. This tightening includes the engine, transmission, u-joints, suspension, dashboard, wheel lugs, whatever you can think of. Now don't get heavy handed about this. Just look about and carefully tighten things. This is a great way to find little problems that, if left unattended, could lead to bigger troubles.

How To Improve Your Car

Once you are settled into a comfortable maintenance schedule, you may want to consider ways of improving your car to a condition even *better* than when it was built. This is not magic, rather the addition of some modern improvements that have come along in recent years.

Probably the *best thing* that can be done for at least 99% of all older cars on the road today is to install a set of *radial tires*. The reason I say 99% is that there are a few old timers that don't take well to radials. But if your car does, the steering and braking improvements can be considerable, and tire wear is generally less rapid. Even the largest of American cars become much more manageable with radial tires. Along with this, larger cars often respond well to heavier duty shock absorbers and new front and rear sway bars. These items will help reduce severe body-roll on turns and excessive pitching and dipping on bumpy roads. Radials, shocks and sway bars won't make larger cars handle like a BMW, but it surely makes them more pleasant to drive.

Many people are interested in improving gas mileage, and there are a number of useful items that may help. An *Electronic Ignition System* such as offered by manufacturers like Mallory, Borg-Warner and Accel, will usually boost mileage figures slightly because they help the engine to stay in-tune longer. Theoretically, without ignition points, the basic timing of an engine cannot change very much, thus the car can go more miles between tune-ups. If you do buy one of these electronic ignition kits, however, be sure to throw your old-fashioned ignition parts in the glove box or trunk, just in case that space-aged black box decides to travel into another dimension while you're in the middle of Wyoming somewhere.

Synthetic Oils, as mentioned earlier, can be a gas saver also if you have a good, tight engine that doesn't leak or burn oil. The synthetic oils allow faster engine warm-up and generally smoother engine operation in all speed ranges. The engine works a little less, and so the gas mileage goes up slightly.

Some major carburetor manufacturers are producing special *gas-saving carburetors* as a means of improving gas mileage on older cars. These carburetors mainly do little more than make the engine run leaner, and this will save gas, but no doubt will cost you power and perhaps some engine life, since leaner engines always run hotter. I don't think I would use a carburetor of this type on any vehicle that is used for heavy service.

Another item worth considering is a *fiberglass fan* to replace the heavy metal one on your car's water pump. Being lighter in weight and more efficient in design, it will theoretically require less horse-power to drive the belt and pulley that operate the fan. It's all quite subtle, of course, but it may make a difference, and as a rule these fiberglass fans cool the engine better. On the minus side, they are more noisy than the stock fan.

An *Electric Fuel Pump* may help both gas mileage and performance, especially if coupled with a *fuel pressure regulator*. The theory here is that the electric pump delivers gas at a steady, even rate, and the pressure regulator ensures that no excessive fuel pressure will be allowed to push beyond the shut-off valve in the carburetor.

For simple and easy maintenance, and a slight benefit in performance, a *foam-type cleanable air filter*, which replaces the disposable, but easily clogged cardboard-oil type found on most cars is worthy of your attention. These foam cleaners, used extensively on racing cars and motorcycles, are merely oil-saturated foam devices that trap airborne dirt particles on an oil film, while allowing generous amounts of clean air to enter the engine. What is nice about these filters is that they can be cleaned and re-used many times, and unlike the older cardboard types, they never swell shut when exposed to moisture.

Exhaust pipe headers and *free-flow exhaust systems* will increase gas mileage and improve your car's performance, but these systems are quite expensive and often illegal to install on most newer cars (because they replace the catalytic converters used in emission control). You might check with your local parts store or dealership about header systems.

On the negative side of things, there are a number of items that *claim* to improve your car, but quite frankly, I cannot see how anything that is poured from a can, other than oil, can do your car much good. Additives are, at best, very temporary solutions to problems that will only get more serious. You cannot replace worn metal or defective seals by opening a can of some hideous glop made in a post office box somewhere. Nor can you suddenly experience a fantastic increase in gas mileage by attaching some magic device that looks like a Martian door knob. I would rather suggest that your car be blessed or danced around or chanted over. No doubt, you'd get as good, or better results and a chuckle over the event as well.

Here are some real improvements that I believe are worth your attention:
1. In-Line Fuel Filter.
2. Transmission oil cooler (especially for automatic cars that tow or do heavy work).
3. Numerical Oil, Amp and Temperature Gauges (to replace the "idiot" light on your dashboard).
4. Back-Up Alarm, which sounds a warning whenever you go into reverse.

5. Improved Headlamps, (Halogen) if permitted in your state.
6. Frost Proof (artic) Windshield Wipers, especially for cars in snow country.
7. Rear Window Defroster Kit (electrical).
8. Lace-On Steering Wheel Cover.
9. Harness-Type Seat Belts.
10. Extra-Large Replacement Rear View Mirror.

Finally, here are the **EIGHT SACRED LAWS OF AUTOMOBILE MAINTENANCE:**

1. It is much easier to take something out than to put it back in.
2. Anything that can go wrong will go wrong (Murphy's Basic Law).
3. Adjustable wrenches are for plumbers, not mechanics.
4. Cheap (bargain) parts don't fit and don't last.
5. If your only tool is a hammer, you'll treat everything like a nail.
6. It's less expensive to repair things *before* they break.
7. Take no advice from strangers.
8. Never touch a car after the sun goes down.

NINE

SAVING MONEY ON PARTS AND REPAIRS

It costs General Motors less than seven cents to produce a spark plug.

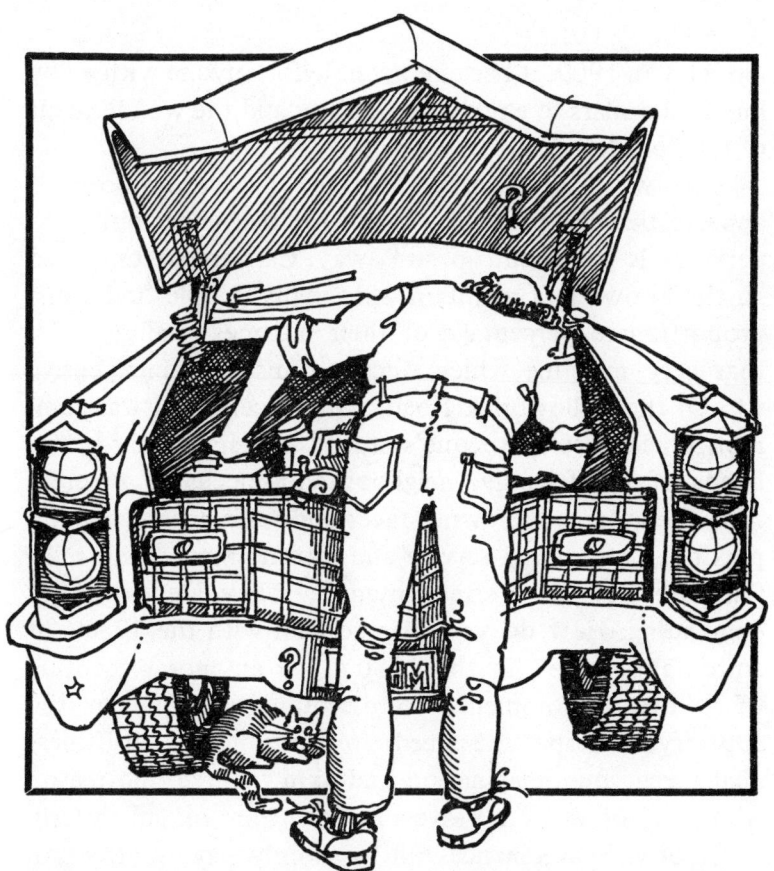

When the first primitive horseless carriages began careening down the dirt roads of America, they frightened livestock, endangered pedestrians, belched with explosions and choked the air with vile, black soot. The general public was harassed and a good deal of criticism ensued from both the local presses and prominent citizens who regarded the horseless carriage as an appalling nuisance, spoiler of tranquility and an instrument of the Devil Himself. All in all, not a bad assessment.

But what these early critics overlooked entirely was the automobile's potential as a great "equalizer" in American society. When Henry Ford began to mass-produce the

Model T in 1909, it became possible for anyone with a few hundred dollars to enjoy the mobility and the wonderment of the horseless carriage.

As we drive together into the 1980's, however, it appears that the price of a ticket for the Automobile Experience is going up, up and away. Cars are becoming so costly to own and maintain that many people find a disproportionate percentage of their incomes swallowed by that very machine which once promised an inexpensive trip on the Yellowbrick Road. Until recently, it was common practice to leave one's sturdy and simple car in the hands of the friendly, neighborhood mechanic, whereas now the average car owner faces endless mechanical complexities, impersonal service and astronomical repair bills. Cars are not so carefree anymore. They are extremely demanding. How do you plan to deal with the "Facts of Automobile Life" in the 1980's? I am not presenting these dreary comments to discourage you. On the contrary, I hope the need for automotive thriftiness challanges your imagination and skill. There's no reason why most of you can't save a full one-third on your yearly automotive maintenance bill by simply paying attention to where you shop and what you buy. This kind of attitude, plus a willingness to "do it yourself" as much as possible (it's easier for some than others, of course), brings personal satisfaction along with valuable information which can be taught to others in your same ecomonic boat.

I am going to use the next few pages to suggest the numerous ways of gaining control over your car's expense account, so you own it and not the other way around. No doubt, some of these suggestions won't fit your particular situation, but survey them all and take note of your needs. If your car is a necessity, so is the rest of this chapter.

Saving Money On Repairs

I. Finding A Good Mechanic

If you happen to know an automobile mechanic who is honest, charges reasonable prices and is never wrong, you have met a truly rare and worthy individual. More often than not, we've all met mechanics who possess one of these characteristics in absence of the others.

I wish I could supply you with some definitive formula for spotting the gifted mechanic; unfortunately, an easy way does not exist. You would think that the mechanic who owns a ten-foot-high tool chest and computerized engine analyzer would be miles ahead of the shabbily dressed person who carries tools in a tackle box or suitcase. However, this type of comparison is equally invalid for mechanics as it is for artists or lawyers. The outward appearace of material success does not guarantee honesty or competence in most societies - - - all that's really implied is a knack for business.

Perhaps a better approach to finding a good mechanic is to consider the type of places where automobiles are repaired. If we try to compare repair facilities with each other, there will be a good deal more statistical information at our disposal than if we try to compare individual mechanics side by side.

For instance, if you were to spend a week or two looking over the files of government and private consumer protection agencies, you would eventually discover two things: first, there are five basic types of automobile repair places, and second, the odds for obtaining competent repair work at a fair price are better in some kinds of shops than in others. Let's look at these ideas more closely for a moment.

If you are a resident in the United States, you have the choice of bringing your car to a gasoline station, a light or heavy speciality shop, a mass merchandiser, an independent garage, or an authorized dealership.

If you happen to choose the gasoline station, the odds are not in your favor for getting the best work, especially if you live in a town populated by more than 50,000 people. The bigger your city, the less likely a gasoline service station will please you. In a very small town or village, a crooked or incompetent mechanic would not survive very long - - - word gets out. This is not the case in sprawling urban centers. For every customer the shoddy mechanic alienates in a day, some stranger will stroll in to replace the lost business.

Generally, a gas station would be an unlikely spot to find a good mechanic. A talented mechanic could earn far better wages elsewhere and would not have to put up with the constant interruptions found in most gas stations. (Again, this is a generalization and does not apply to every gas station in America. We're still talking about odds; and for every ten people who get a poor repair job, a few may be quite satisfied. No matter how bad the odds, there are always a few winners. Think of all the people who made it off the Titanic!). More often than not, gas stations are training grounds for the "learn as you go" type of mechanic. This is understandable considering the lack of training facilities for mechanics in the United States. Of course, if you hear of a gas station mechanic with a fantastic reputation, by all means, check it out. But if you're just going in blind, statistics show that, by far, the most complaints received by private and government consumer bureaus are connected with local gas stations.

If you drive into a specialty shop, either light (such as

brakes or mufflers), or heavy (such as transmisssions), your chances for a satisfactory repair job aren't much better. The problem with specialty shops is twofold: one, they are usually franchises, often run by an absentee owner who is interested in large sales volume, and two, these shops frequently try to solve every car problem in terms of what they sell. In other words, if you go to a muffler shop because your car makes funny noises, you'll probably get a muffler even though the exhaust system may have nothing to do with the noise.

Specialty shops are as much concerned with selling as with fixing. It's quite likely that the same person who courteously listens to your problems while writing up the repair ticket, is also making a percentage on everything he or she sells you. Therefore, my advice is similar to that offered about gas stations - - - you must be able to verify the business record and competence level of a shop before you go in. See if you can talk to some other customers of the shop. You might also try to find out who fixes transmissions on the local police or public works vehicles, and who does specialty muffler work on locally owned race cars. Sometimes, your local Better Business Bureau (which is, by the way, supported by business, not by the government), or District Attorney's Office will tell you if a certain shop has been a serious problem to them. They will not, however, tell you if that shop has only a few complaints against it. This is only fair, considering that some customers' complaints are very unreasonable. There are losers on both sides of the fence, you know.

The third type of repair shop is the *familiar mass merchandiser,* which includes such places as Sears and Roebuck, Montgomery Ward, K-Mart, Woolco, Times Square Stores, Grand Auto, etc. These stores offer a wide range of services, and while they aren't the very best in what they do, they are far from the worst. The main benefit to the patron of the mass-merchandiser is that he will always have someplace to complain. These large chains are very image-concious, and will generally attempt to satisfy their customers to a much larger extent than some small-time gas station. The repair work in these service centers ranges from very good to a bit sloppy, and the quality of what you get often depends on the kind of car you own. If it's a popular American make, chances are that they will put the brakes on properly and point the muffler in the right direction. But if it's a Datsun or a Volvo, it may get the same kind of treatment as an American car, and your little foreign puppy may wimper and protest as a result. If it's a less popular foreign make, like a Fiat, Renault or Jaguar, no problem; they won't even let you in the door. Another difficulty to be aware of is the questionable quality of the parts used by the less prestigious mass merchandisers. Probably, of all the big chain operations, Sears or Montgomery Ward would be the best bet for getting satisfaction and reasonable quality, however, not necessarily the lowest price.

The *independent garages* offer the best chance, statistically, of getting a good job at a fair price; only because they are cheaper than the authorized dealerships. If the authorized dealers didn't charge such high prices for repair work (over $40 per hour in some cities), the complaint rate would probably be about the same for the independent specialist as for the dealer. These independent garages are, by the way, usually shops that fix only certain kinds of cars; either just one make (like VW's) or cars imported from one country (like Japan). I would be wary of a garage that "specializes" in twenty different makes of cars. These independent garages do not sell gas or new cars; and if they've been in business for a number of years, that's another good sign. Of course, they can be just as rotten as the worst gas station, but as a rule, many of these specialized shops demonstrate a good deal of competence and fairness. The message here is the same as before. Seek out their reputation. Has the shop been around for a long time? Is it a family business? Do you know someone with a car just like yours who has had repairs done at this shop? Sometimes, a visit to these independent shops before admitting your car for repairs would be a good idea. Ask some questions about their training and facilities. If they take the time to show you around and introduce you to other mechanics working there, it may be the start of a nice relationship. If they are brusque, rude or suspicious, they may be incompetents or just eccentric geniuses. "Everything in life is a risk", as we clever people like to say; but *remember the odds* - - - Harry's VW garage is always a better risk than the Kung Fu Petroleum Company.

Are you surprised that authorized dealerships aren't the most frequent recipients of consumer complaints? In general, the quality of their repairs is favorable (although many consumers do complain about the high prices). This trend is closely tied to the type of car produced over the past ten years. The intricacies of the modern automobile require expensive tools and testing equipment that only the biggest and most prosperous shops can afford. For instance, it is extremely difficult, if not impossible, to repair most new cars without the use of an exhaust analyzer; and a good one doesn't come cheap (a few thousand dollars). Therefore, it shouldn't be difficult to predict that the authorized dealerships will have a monopolistic grip upon auto repair profits within the next few years. The law of the auto repair business for the

1980's is already being sounded loud and clear: *Attention, all garages! Get Big or get out!*

In summary, good mechanics are a rare breed, the result of a domineering auto industry. Anyone, *anyone* can procure a business license and simply start fixing cars. Presumably, a twelve year old junior high school student could open up shop in most states, and perhaps do a decent job, come to think of it. I would rather spend more money with a licensed mechanic and have the work done properly, than spend fewer dollars more frequently for wasted and unnecessary repairs.

A common image, often perpetrated by the popular media, is that many mechanics are 'conniving little thieves'. This is a fallacy. Some of them just don't know very much, and occasionally find themselves in situations which require a little larceny to get out of. They spend a great deal of time guessing and if they're wrong, you pay. I would say that premediated fraud only occurs, possibly, 10% of the time. Most rip-offs are unplanned, a kind of unintentional thievery brought about by a mechanic's error in judgement.

What every car owner would like to find is a mechanic who is both honest and skillful. Never begrudge spending money on repair work when your car is in such capable hands. In the long run, it's a bargain.

II. Fixing It Yourself

In response to the high cost, and often poor quality of auto repair, many people are getting involved, to some degree, with their own repair work. Some venture only to change the oil and filter and replace a fuse now and then; others take it one step further and attempt tune-ups, brakes, fan belts, hoses and gaskets; a few go all the way and devote many hours of study and learning to the final conquest of the machine that has cost them so much time, money and grief.

There are a number of ways to learn the art of fixing your own car, depending upon how deeply you want to approach the whole business. A knowledgable friend can teach you the rudiments of an oil change and a weekly check under the hood. Many communities have local vocational schools, alternative universities, and community colleges which offer classes ranging from basic familiarization to a very thorough one or two year course in auto repair. There are also numerous books and other aids available on the subject, again from the very basic to the highly technical. I will tell you more about these in a moment.

When you embark upon your journey into the mysterious world of automotive repair, it is important to understand that fixing a car takes a lot of skill, physical strength and patience. If your community school is offering courses, be aware that classes meeting only once a week over a period of a month or two are only *familiarization courses*. Many schools, quite unintentionally, mislead people about how much can be accomplished in a short time. I've seen descriptions such as: "In a few weeks' time, you will have a thorough understanding of how your car works . . ." This is nonsense. In a few weeks, you'll know where to *find* all the components of your car, which is a great first step, but you won't know how to fix them. It is essential that you set realistic goals if you plan to become a fix-it-yourself-er. If you want to learn car repair so precisely that you'll never need the services of a mechanic, plan on devoting as much time to auto mechanics as you would to a few college level physics course. Look upon your car for what it is -- the product of a very sophisticated technology that cannot be understood and mastered overnight.

I learned auto mechanics by the Lower East Side Montessori Method - - I just started taking cars apart. I realize that this approach may be a bit radical, so I would suggest a more modest beginning. For openers, I recommend enrolling in a basic familiarization course. Once you've crawled around in all that grease for a while, gotten a few shovelfuls of dirt in your eyes and reduced your hands to the Paws of Frankenstein, you may decide that auto mechanics is ok, *but* not so very much fun after all, except on the fundamental level of routine maintenance work. That's just fine because, at this point, one of the many good automotive books on the market could be very useful. Here are just a few you might check-out at a local bookstore or library. If you don't have easy access to either place, just drop a line to the publisher. I've also included a few of the more advanced books for those who intend to push beyond the basic maintenance level. These should probably be read while learning mecanics from a night class or friend.

Chilton's Easy Car Care, Chilton's Books, Radnor, Penn. 19089.

This is a good book for learning basic maintenance and automotive theory. It's very thorough and has pictures for guiding you through different kinds of checks and repairs.

How To Keep Your Volkswagen Alive, John Muir Publications, P.O. Box 613 Sante Fe, New Mexico 87501.

Most of you have probably heard of John Muir's famous book for beginners who want to tear their Volkswagens apart. Amazingly enough, most beginners succeed admirably in everything from brake work to engine rebuilding. A funny, friendly book that will teach a great deal.

Economy Driving, H.P. Books, Box 5367, Tucson, AZ 85703.

H.P. Books puts out a number of interesting titles. This one tells about the facts and myths of gas mileage and how you can improve it. The book is very technical, yet understandable for the most part, even if your experience with cars is minimal. Not for the absolute beginner, but a good book for a little later on in your mechanical career. H.P. also has a book on handling and suspension systems, among others.

Motor Auto Repair Manuals, 1790 B'Way, New York, N.Y. 10019.

The Motor's Manuals for American automobiles is updated every year and includes repair sections for cars up to seven years old. These manuals are not for the beginner, but would be ok for the serious tinkerer. These books assume you know quite a bit about automotive terminology.

Clymer's Auto Repair Manuals, 222 No. Virgil Ave. L.A., Calif. 90004.

Clymer's publishes individual manuals for a wide range of foreign and domestic cars and motorcycles. These books are techical in nature and not for the novice; however, if your're a novice and you own a weird or unpopular car, you might buy one anyway just in case you break down in some strange place where no info on your type of car is readily available to the local mechanic.

How to Get Your Car Repaired, Margaret Bresnahan Carlson, Harrow Books.

I don't recommend this book for it's mechanical advice, which is often misleading; however, it does contain an excellent section on where to go, or write, or call, in order to complain about poorly done repairs.

Why Trade It In?, George and Suzanne Fremon, Strait and Company.

Although this book is advertised primarily as a guide to keeping a used car going strong, I think it has excellent sections on the workings of a car and how to troubleshoot automotive problems on your own. A good book for learning some basic automotive theroy.

The Automobile In America, Stephen Sears, American Heritage Books, New York, N.Y.

An excellent and highly readable book about the past, present and future of the automobile. If you're at all interested in the car as culture, you will enjoy Sears' book immensely.

Saving Money On Parts and Repairs 137

In addition, if you need just about any book on any car (including the old timers), drop a line to : Mr. David Moe, Milestone Motor Co., 2411 California St., San Francisco, California 94115. Repair manuals are also available through the J.C. Whitney and Co. catalog, 1917 Archer Avenue, Chicago, Illinois 60680.

One last suggestion: if you really want to teach yourself a good deal about cars in a short period of time, you might consider model-building. The Revell Corporation makes a plastic model called the "Visible V-8" (available in most hobby stores). This is a very realistic miniature of a car engine and actually runs on batteries. It is a bit difficult to assemble, and ironically, requires about the same amount of patience and skill as the real thing. As of this printing, the cost hovers around $22.00 (glue and batteries not included), and comes with a nifty little book which describes the workings of the internal combustion engine as well as other componenets of the modern automobile. If you successfully construct this model, or even get it together and it doesn't spin very well, you will have learned things that some mechanics don't even know. You'll be able to throw around terms like *valve job, cam shaft* and *timing gear*. Mystify your friends and gain new popularity! Plan to spend about five evenings on this project, and if your kit happens to have an extra battery contact button, send it to me because I didn't get one.

Saving Money On Parts

Most repair shops, with the exception of certain chain stores, charge full list price for their parts, although they obtain them at a substantial discount. Unless you do your own car work, there's not much you can do about this situation since very few repair shops allow you to supply the parts.

However, if you decide to do some work on your own (such as oil change, battery installation, windshield wipers, antifreeze or headlights), you can save quite a bit of money if you know where to find the best prices. Here are some suggestions:

1. Mass Merchandisers

The big chain stores mentioned earlier in this chapter are excellent places to shop for maintenance items such as oil, filters, shocks, wiper blades, hosed, belts, fuses, bulbs, batteries, tires, greases, solvents and tools. Of course, the selection is somewhat limited to American and a few popular foreign car products (VW or Japanese makes), but you will find the prices considerably below those of authorized dealerships, auto supply stores and gas stations. Frequently, these stores also provide installation of their products at very reasonable labor rates.

2. Local Auto Supply Stores

Auto supply stores, also known as independent jobbers, are the main source of parts for most gas stations and independent garages since they undersell the authorized dealer while offering a good selection of products. They also tend to be the most helpful among the different types of parts outlets. I will often spend a little more by shopping at a local auto supply store, but I appreciate the personal service. At least, if they don't have something, they will try to order it by the next day. I like that.

3. Authorized Dealerships

I'm mentioning authorized dealerships briefly here, not because they offer any bargains (hardly!), only because it is wisest to buy certain items from them exclusively especially if you own a foreign car. In particular, I refer to gaskets. When you get them from a dealer, they always fit. Whereas it can be a terrible nuisance trying to fit one from another source. This could be related to the age of the gaskets on the shelf. Anyway, it's a tip worth noting.

4. Wrecking Yards

Wrecking yards can be an excellent source for saving money if you use them in the right way. First of all, before you shop for a used part, find out how much a new or rebuilt one would cost. It often happens that the wrecking yard price is almost as much as a new part would cost. For instance, it is possible to find shiny, new carburetors for older VW's on sale for about $40. So, don't let a wrecking yard have $25 for a filthy, old one.

Another way to save yourself and the yard people a lot of aggravation is to have certain information about your car in hand. You should be able to tell the wrecker people the year, make, model, engine size and type of transmission. If your request is something like "I need a power steering pump for a 1965 Ford Mustang with a 289 V-8 and 4 speed transmission", it will always be appreciated. This will also insure your membership in the "club" of regular and welcome customers. (When you feel courageous enough, you can even use words like "tranny" and "fourbanger", but don't try to climb the social ladder too fast). A good idea would be to compile all this information on an index card for storage in your glovebox--next to your gloves.

And last, but not least, please keep in mind that there are some items that no junk yard likes to mess around with. If you go in asking for one radio knob, or the letter "D" for your Dodge, they will hate you. Wait until you buy something big, then ask for the smaller stuff. You'll probably get it for free. Also, avoid asking for items which are available anywhere for just a few dollars, like shocks, break shoes or a fan belt. Use the wrecking yard for parts that are difficult to find or very expensive to buy elsewhere. Auto wreckers do make a lot of money, but they work hard for it. Make their day a little easier. In turn, they will do wonders for you.

5. The Local Newspaper

Check the "Auto Parts" section of the Automotive Classifieds in your local paper. Many times, people are selling their extra parts or entire cars at bargain rates.

6. Mail Order Catalogs

The most famous of all automotive mail order catalogs is put out by J.C. Whitney and Company, 1917 Archer Avenue, Chicago, Illinois, 60680. They carry an incredible array of stuff, from the practical to the bizarre, and the prices and service are generally quite good. Certainly, shipping errors can occur, but Whitney's is quick to satisfy the disgruntled, and I can speak from personal experience. Most often, I use Whitney's for unusual items that are hard to find. Most orders are filled between ten days and two weeks.

Both Sears Roebuck and Montgomery Ward offer service from their catalogs, but you might find prices not really in the bargain category. It's more of a convenience service for those who aren't close to a supply of auto parts.

A Word On Parts Guarantees

Wherever you choose to buy parts, be sure to ask the limits of the guarantee. Most automobile parts are now guaranteed for 90 days, although many items purchased from an authorized dealer have one-year guarantee. Some items require installation by selling company, and on many types of electrical equipment, there are all kinds of restrictions and disclaimers. Check all of this out before you buy, including whatever you get from a wrecking yard.

TEN

THE AUTOMOTIVE INDUSTRY AND YOU

> Big corporations fix prices among themselves and drive out the small entrepreneur. In their conglomerate forms, the huge corporations have begun to challenge the legitimacy of the state.
>
> —Gore Vidal

It is no secret that a large number of American car owners are thoroughly fed-up with the automobile industry. Poor quality control, shoddy and ill-conceived designs, expensively disappointing dealer services, incompetent or dishonest repair shops . . . you name it, the automobile industry has done it all. How in the world have things gotten so bad?

The answer to the economic chaos and exploitive nature of the automobile industry is hardly a simple one, but it is worth some time to think about. As a car owner, the more you know about how the collective, entire automotive system works, the better your chances for dealing with it on a day to day basis.

It's very hard to believe that once, maybe fifty years ago, the auto industry, and Henry Ford in particular, was highly regarded as a positive and beneficial force in our society. Not only had the ingenious Mr. Ford (for all his faults, he *was* ingenious) broken the isolation of millions of rural Americans with his famous Model T, but the industry, in general, had provided an often inexpensive and yet high quality "magic carpet on wheels" for all of us to ride in search of the good life. It wasn't, in fact, until much later, in the late 1950's and early

1960's that people began to notice the smog hovering above Los Angeles and the tragic loss of over 70,000 Americans yearly in automobile accidents.

Following the lead of public interest crusaders like Ralph Nader and the innovative state government of California, the Federal Government, at long last, decided to take decisive steps toward solving the serious problems being caused by the proliferating automobile. It was thought that a compromise could be reached, that somewhere between the extremes of corporate greed without conscience and stifling government intervention, the great American auto industry would come to rest. It would be improved yet still remain prosperous; an industrial machine of immense power, yet still a business responsive to the safety and well-being of the ten million or so Americans who buy new cars annually.

Looking today at the records of private and government consumer protection agencies, however, it seems that the auto industry is more of an enemy than a friend. Automobile-related complaints are by far the most frequent problem in virtually every District Attorney's office and Better Business Bureau in the nation. Recall campaigns (over 12 million cars in 1977, 9 million in 1978!) and class action law suits (the Ford Pinto, Firestone 500 radial tires) have been a familiar part of the national news. The labor rate for everyday auto repairs in some cities now exceeds $40 per hour. Minor collisions between newer cars run up repair bills into the hundreds and even thousands of dollars. Insurance rates are prohibitive. All in all, it looks as if something has to change quickly, or a large number of poor and even not-so-poor Americans are simply going to have to abandon their cars for lack of money or skill to keep them going. Are such drastic consequences inevitable?
in sight to the ills of the auto industry?

Most automotive industry executives think that the cure lies with the culprit who first caused the disease—the Federal Government. Pressured by the demands of unreasonable and unknowledgeable consumer groups, the government has put the auto industry in an impossible situation, or so the automobile people insist. The Federal regulations concerning exhaust emissions are "arbitrary" and "scientifically unsound" according to some automotive engineers, and their argument does have some merit. Less believable is the auto industry's protest against mandatory passive restraints and air bags as "overly expensive" and a "nuisance". The government's reply to this is that the auto industry has chosen to make a rather large profit on safety equipment, and thus the excessive cost is their own problem. A third objection often raised by the auto industry is the government's insistence on stricter gas mileage requirements. These standards mandate the industry to produce a fleet of cars by 1985 that will average no less than 27.5 miles per gallon. Aside from the technical impossibilities of these requirements, the companies argue that it would be far better to abandon, or relax, these ideal standards because of "public pressure". Market surveys reveal that Americans don't want small, uncomfortable cars, as they did during the Oil Crisis of 1973. Likewise, car manufacturers claim that the people do not want the elaborate safety features either. Instead, consumers want a desireable car to drive of their free choice, and not one prescribed by government standards.

The federal government is indeed exerting considerable pressure on the auto industry as the result of the growing political power of consumer groups throughout the country and, of course, in response to the growing energy crisis. There is little doubt that the automobile was overdue for regulation of some kind as evidence increased yearly that private automobiles were consuming great amounts of fossil fuel, causing undue deaths, and adding mightily to the brown industrial clouds that crown our glittering American cities. At dead-center of what bothers many people about the government's actions, however, is that the public is suddenly being told to do the opposite of what it has been since WWII! Through media, consumers have been encouraged, cajoled and even coerced to enjoy and buy almost everything in sight. After some 30 years of this hype, we are now being told that frugality and economy must be our primary goal; *even if the cost of frugality is higher than the previous behavior of blind consumption.* It seems that the American consumer is the one stuck with the bills for the energy crisis. The government legislates, the auto manufacturers complain, the oil companies profit, and the consumer pays for it all.

An interesting viewpoint on the ills of the auto industry comes from the people that consumers come most often in contact with, the auto mechanic. Mechanics feel that they are the *only* scapegoat in a power game that is far beyond their influence. Their job has little prestige in the U.S., unlike as in Europe or Japan, yet being an auto mechanic is easily one of the most difficult of all "trades" in our society. A mechanic who is employed by a dealership, for instance, is pressured to "beat the clock" on auto repairs. If that weren't bad enough, automobiles being produced today are so complex that mechanics must spend many hours studying and struggling with new intricate mechanical systems. Even the independent garage or gas station owner cannot find much consolation in having to spend most of a day in fixing cars that have been built deliberately to break and be thrown away. Mechanics know better than anyone else the blazing truth about the auto business (a truth many car owners are ignorant of) — the only money to be made in the car world is in the making and selling of automobiles, not fixing them honestly.

The average car owner doesn't know who to scream at first. We are furious with the manufacturers who designed our automobile so poorly, and at the union workers who slammed it together (they aren't paid to work carefully) angry with the dealer who sold it, disgusted with the mechanic who can't fix it, and filled with remorse for ever having bought it. About the only people in this unfortunate chain of errors who escape the public wrath are the ones who deserve a good deal of it — the myth-makers who write the ads for the automobile industry.

I think the general public would be much more accepting of todays intricate and expensive automobiles if they at least were given what was promised to them— the safest and most reliable cars ever to ride the roads of America. But most of us don't believe this is the case. We see that a new car can be torn apart with bare hands. In fact, it happens unintentionally all the time. And reliabiblity? Well, the record speaks for itself everytime we see a 20 year old car cruising faithfully past our broken down 3 year old models.

Do modern automobiles really have to be poorly manufactured plastic boxes in order to meet government safty and emission standards? Or is the automobile industry taking the American public for a ride? Considering today's automobile, it is doubtful that the car manufacturers are really concerned with the welfare of the people who buy their products.

What's ahead in the next twenty years for the automobile is anybody's guess, but one would hope that new technological breakthroughs might help to alleviate some of the problems. First of all, a new type of engine, hopefully electric, could gradually replace the gasoline and diesel-powered car in heavily populated urban areas. Secondly, new and efficient forms of public transportation could encourage people to drive less, and in fact, could even change the physical appearance of our cities and countryside, slaves that they now are to the needs of the automobile.

Until these two breakthroughs occur, you as a car owner will undoubtedly face more and more expensive operating costs. Gasoline prices will surely go up. Diesel fuel will also increase in price considerably, and soon fuel will also increase in price considerably, and soon Federal restrictions on the rather filthy exhaust emissions coming from diesel engines will eliminate the diesel car. The cost of repairs and spare parts for automobiles of all types will also spiral upward. In fact, unless you either start to fix your own car or start to make lots more money, you're a dead duck in the automotive department. People with older autos will fare slightly better than those who own late 70's or early 80's cars because the older ones will be easier to repair and will generally last longer. Hopefully, by the time we reach the bleak point when all the older cars are completely worn out, and the newer ones have fallen apart during attempts to get more than 50,000 miles out of them, perhaps some nifty new personal vehicle (not nuclear powered, please) or efficient aerobus will be there to take care of most of us. In any event, we are all changing our thinking about cars, and our reasons for driving them. Let's face it. The good old days of hitting the road just for the hell of it are slowly coming to a close.

Appendix A

Questions People Always Ask Me

Q: *Have you ever been stuck with a "lemon" used car?*

A: Yes, but only in my inexperienced younger days. This book is, after all, the product of all my own mistakes, as well as those of everyone who told me their sad stories. As the quality of my information and mechanical skills have increased, no lemon has knocked on by door.

Q: *What will the cars of the 1980's be like?*

A: My guess is that they will continue along the trend of becoming smaller and having the "wedge-type" design. The cars for the 1980's will be highly technical in their design, utilizing electronics, plastic and lightweight metals. They will undoubtedly increase in price, and will be difficult and expensive to repair. One of the greatest problems for the automotive industry during the 80's will be to make cars that are small and efficient, yet reasonably safe in case of accident.

Toward the end of the decade, it's possible that we will see a reasonably good electric car of modest driving range and performance, suitable for big city commuting. Here again, one solution will create another new problem, namely, from where can we get the energy to charge-up millions of these electric cars every day?

Q: *If you were going to buy a new car, what would it be?*
A: I seriously doubt if I would ever buy a new car, since it seems like such a poor investment. But if I did have a change of heart, I would probably buy a Japanese make; a *Dodge/Omni,* or *Plymouth Horizon.*
   There are a number of other appealing choices among the Japanese cars. *Datsun* and *Honda* look good because they run on regular gas and may help to avoid possible price and supply problems in the near future. The *Toyota* has the best styling, especially the *Celica Liftback.* This is the first Toyota I've seen that doesn't look like a toaster of the future.
   The *Dodge/Omni,* as well as its companion, the *Plymouth Horizon* are modeled after the *Honda Civic* and the *VW Rabbit,* both having a front wheel drive design with a side-ways engine. The *Omni* has received some unfavorable reviews from consumer groups, and I wish the media hadn't made such a big deal about it. Every new model has its bugs, and I would be disappointed if the public withdrew its support for this car with its noteworthy engineering concept. Already GM is marketing its *Chevy Citation* which has a similar mechanical design.

Q: *What type of car do you drive?*
A: I change cars quite a bit in order to get experience with the many different kinds. Right now I'm driving a 1971 *Toyota Corolla* that I bought from a used car lot in San Francisco for $345. It looks rundown, but after about $100 in miscellaneous repairs, the car is proving to be very reliable in both city and cross-country driving. My one complaint is that I can't carry very much in it. With one suitcase, a cantaloupe, and a ferocious cat, it's very tight in there!

Appendix B

 Autobiographies

If you're wondering who's the big cheese in the auto manufacturing business in America, a quick glance upon General Motors should answer your question. As of the first quarter of 1979, GM has cornered about sixty-four per cent (64%) of the entire domestic car market. This is probably discouraging to the competition, especially to American Motors which now owns about 1.8% of the market. There's nothing like the spirit of free competition! And by the way, don't be too upset if you notice little defects here and there in your new GM car. After all, some of these autos are produced at a rate of 100 per hour!

Did somebody mention defects? How about poor Robert Armour of San Francisco? He picked up his brand new car at 7:30 one sunny morning, and 4 hours later his wheel fell off at a busy intersection. Not bad for 56 miles!

At a time when there's a good deal of interest in "alternative" types of automobiles, people might be surprised to learn that there is a steam car in America capable of going 1,500 miles on only 24 gallons of water. The car produces 76 h.p., accelerates briskly, and is of such high quality that a 36 month guarantee is in the glove box.

Don't plan on buying one, though; unfortunately the company is already out of business. But you can see this remarkable car by visiting the Henry Ford Museum in Dearborn, Michigan. Look for the 1925 Doble Model E.

The next time you read or see some egotistical advertisement for a new make of automobile, you might keep in mind that there's a tendency in our society toward technological snobbery. Not only do books, films and TV shows fail to give credit to the American Indians for building pyramids and having a diverse technology, but our advertising media tries to pass along the impression that *no one* in the history of the world has ever been as clever as their clients, the sponors.

Here's just a small list of accomplishments in automotive technology that happened before many of us were born (me included):

> The pneumatic automobile tire......1895
> Front-wheel drive................1897
> Adjustable steering wheel..........1902
> Superchargers....................1902
> Four-wheel drive.................1904
> The V-8 engine...................1905
> The Automatic Transmission........1936
> The Fault-Free Automobile.. Undiscovered

Less than one in five drivers (18.5%) use seatbelts, according to the National Highway Safety Administration. Drivers are more "safety-minded" in the West (23.7%), and women use their belts more often (20.6%) than men. The city of Seattle scores highest, with over 33% of its drivers using seat belts. As for use in particular types of cars, Volvo drivers buckled up at a rate of 14.6% and Cadillac owners threw caution to the wind by scoring only 14%.

SOME AUTOMOTIVE FIRSTS

The first automobile to go coast-to-coast was a Winton driven by Dr. Horatio Nelson Jackson and his mechanic Sewell Crocker. They struggled from San Francisco to New York in just over 60 days, in 1903.

In 1909, Alice Ramsey became the first woman to complete the journey across America. In 1977, it was reported that she was alive and well at 90, living in California and still driving a car.

The first automobile fatality in New York City occurred on September 13, 1899, when a real estate salesman named Bliss was run over near Central Park. There is no truth to the rumor that a taxicab was involved.

The first gasoline car in America was the Duryea, built in 1893; however, it failed to work properly, so credit should be given for the first successful gasoline car in the U.S., the Haynes, built in 1904.

The number of automobiles in the U.S. is still growing at an alarming rate. In 1900, there were 8,000; in 1938 it was 25 million, and in 1979 the number was at nearly 110 million. By the year 2000, it might be a bit crowded.

A random government sampling of some 200 cars in six states revealed that almost 70% of them have altered or defective emission-control systems.